REVENUE 20/20:
Back to Basics

Kristin Rollison

Revenue 20/20: Back to Basics
Kristin Rollison

© 2021 Kristin Rollison. All rights reserved.

Published in 2021 by Kristin Rollison with the assistance of Publicious Book Publishing
www.publicious.com.au

This book is for educational purposes only. The author claims no responsibility to any person or entity for any liability, loss, or damage caused or alleged to be caused directly or indirectly as a result of the use, application, or interpretation of the information presented herein. Before acting on this information, you should consider the appropriateness of the advice in regard to your own situation.

The moral right of the author to be identified as the author of this work has been asserted.

All rights reserved. No part of this document may be reproduced or transmitted in any form or by any means, electronic, mechanical, photocopying, recording or otherwise, or by any information storage and retrieval system, without prior written permission of Kristin Rollison or publisher (except by a reviewer, who may quote brief passages and/or show brief video clips in a review).

For permissions:
Revenue 20/20 email: info@revenue2020.com
https://www.revenue2020.com/

Prepublication Data Service Details available from:
the National Library of Australia
ISBN 978-0-6452785-0-7 (paperback)
ISBN: 978-0-6452785-1-4 (eBook)

The author has made every effort to contact copyright holders for material used in this book. Any person or organisation that may have been overlooked should contact the author or publisher.

Cover photograph by Julia Molodeva
Cover design and book layout by
Publicious Book Publishing
www.publicious.com.au

"What do we live for, if not to make life less difficult for each other?" – George Eliot

TABLE OF CONTENTS

WELCOME	1
CHAPTER 1: FUNDAMENTALS	7
Transferrable Skills	7
Economic Trends & Cycles	7
Perishable Inventory	8
So… What is Revenue Management?	9
Where Did Revenue Management Come From?	10
Who is a Revenue Manager?	11
Art vs. Science	11
Integration	12
CHAPTER 2: COMMUNICATION	14
Words Over Numbers?	14
Know Your Audience (and when to shut up)	18
In Writing	18
In Print	20
Cut the Fluff	20
In Person	20
If you Don't Know, THEN ASK	21
The Objective of Meetings	22

CHAPTER 3: ANALYTICS — 23

    The Importance of Numbers — 23

    Daily Habits — 23

    Analysis Paralysis — 25

    Healthy Boundaries — 27

    Science vs. Art — 28

    Incremental Revenue — 34

    Revenue Management Software — 35

    Outsource Analytics — 38

CHAPTER 4: UNDERSTANDING YOUR BUSINESS — 39

    The Basics — 39

    Supply & Demand — 42

    Producers — 42

    Consumers — 44

    Budgets & Forecasts — 45

    Base Business — 49

CHAPTER 5: PRICING & PRODUCT — 51

    Know Your Worth — 52

    Market Research — 54

    Pricing — 55

    Static & Dynamic — 56

    Static — 58

    Dynamic — 60

    Product — 61

    The Product — 61

    Packages & Promotions — 63

Packages	63
Promotions	66
Airbnb	68
The Price is Right	70

CHAPTER 6: DISTRIBUTION — 71

Sources	72
Channels	73
Why It Matters	74
Segmentation	75
Control Your Inventory	76
Rate Parity	78
Why It Matters	80
Complications	82
Keep it simple, know where you're selling your rooms *and why*.	84
Control	84

CHAPTER 7: LOYALTY — 87

Bigger Fish in the Pond	91
Read Reviews	92
Be a Lobby Lizard	93
Don't Assume	93
Guest Complaints	95
Loyalty in Customer Service	99
Marketing & PR	99
Outsourcing Loyalty	101
Commerce	102

CHAPTER 8: TRAINING & DEVELOPMENT — 107
- Teach Everyone Everything — 107
- Recruiting — 108
- The Measure of Quality — 109
- Set Up for Success — 110
- Think Outside the Building — 113
- Outsource Training — 114

CHAPTER 9: OUTSOURCING — 117
- Management Agreements — 126
- Resources — 130
- Local Brands — 131
- Global Brands — 133
- Independent Alliances — 135
- The Takeaway — 136

CHAPTER 10: CONCLUSION — 138

ACKNOWLEDGEMENTS — 142

REFERENCES — 144

ABOUT THE AUTHOR — 146

WELCOME

'Revenue management...'

Although the concept was coined by the hotel industry decades ago, 'revenue management' is not a unique practice. Originally adapted from the airline's pricing and capacity process, called 'yield management', today it is a fundamental backbone for all forms of accommodation. The more these practices have evolved, the more apparent it has become that the theories behind both strategies are universal to most economic sectors around the world—understand your supply and demand, then price accordingly to maximize revenue.

Simple.

And yet so complex.

This book may be in your hands right now, *at this very moment*, because you want to better manage the art and science of revenue management at your hotel, or in your life. Maybe you're a learning enthusiast, curious about a career in the numbers field, or how to translate these hospitality practices into your industry. Perhaps you're a property owner wondering how else to improve your financial outlook, especially now as we find our way through a global pandemic. Whether by upskilling your team, outsourcing your problems, broadening your reach, or signing on with a management group, you'll find various perspectives to help you make those decisions.

If you're a hospitality student, these chapters provide a high-level lens into the top-line-money-generating world that is revenue, helping you decide if you want to dive into a career in revenue (P.S. - we would love you to!)

Lastly, at a hotel level, this book can aid General Managers in determining if help is required with their strategies, or if, as captain of their ship, they've already built a smooth sailing, full-steam-ahead vessel.

Who am I to teach you about any of this? Great question!

I have worked my entire adult life in hotels and revenue management. I learned from a team of seasoned experts at a school in Switzerland, refined my service skills interning at The Lausanne Palace, then began my hospitality career in the *city of hotels*, Las Vegas. The Westin was my first exposure to working for the huge international hotel chain that was Starwood, now part of Marriott International. I fumbled my way through on-the-job learning in every department until I fully understood how all the parts fit together to make the engine work; it was an amazing knowledge building experience.

I landed in revenue management while covering a maternity leave vacancy. I was young and energetic, convinced that overseeing front office operations at the same time as revenue and reservations would be manageable. Ha! I was soon aware of how much work was involved in these roles, and how pleasingly extensive my impact on revenue growth was, and could be, if I gave it all my focus. I was obsessed. I fell in love with the numbers and stepped out of the front office and into a solely focused role as Director of Revenue. I would create analyses that helped me understand how much demand Las Vegas was seeing, and how to price our rooms accordingly. And then—how to push that rate out into the World Wide Web for everyone to see, and book, and stay! It was amazing! The possibilities were endless, and I was brimming with ideas.

A few years later, I was recruited by Caesars Entertainment group to revenue manage the Flamingo Las Vegas Hotel & Casino. This was my first exposure to being part of a centralized team structure, where all the hotel's revenue managers worked out of one office. I missed the pulse of the day-to-day encounters with guests and staff by not working so closely with the hotel operations, but I did gain enormous experience in managing multiple Godzilla-sized properties simultaneously. I honed my skills in both pricing and forecasting, and in understanding the casino-related market segments, learning how to leverage each of them for optimal *overall* revenue, not just rooms.

Eventually, I found my happy place with the MGM Resorts International group, as Director of Revenue Operations at The Mirage Hotel & Casino. My office was behind the front desk, and I could truly live and breathe the pulse of the business and guests firsthand again, while working as a team with the other hotels, collaborating with my counterparts and the properties they each managed within the MGM group. Sadly, my time there was short-lived as my husband and I were offered an opportunity to relocate to Australia for him to help with the rebranding project of Sydney's only casino hotel at that time, The Star. It was about to undergo an $860 million dollar transformation, and with his experience in opening the restaurants at Vegas' newest gem City Centre, The Star's Managing Director knew my husband could help. We packed up the house and our dogs and flew across the Pacific to our next adventure.

I began my new role as Group Director of Revenue for the largest publicly traded Australian hotel company, EVENT Hospitality & Entertainment. As I met everyone in the group, I could see how well our work ethics and values aligned, I knew we were a good fit for each other. With fifty or so hotels to help manage at the time, I was able to impact them both strategically and by being hands on as well. I provided the revenue teams with training, support, and best practices, while also able to tactically step in and assist the identified 'need' hotels too. There was always an opportunity to help.

I had always yearned to contribute more broadly to the hotel industry as a whole and not just to one group, so after nearly ten years of working for EVENT, when I was given that chance, I took it. It was mere weeks before the 2020 pandemic emerged in full force, and coincidentally my role was made redundant as my responsibilities had been combined with another position during my maternity leave. While parting ways was bittersweet, in hindsight and with the COVID aftermath that ensued, I know I dodged a big bullet. I now had the opportunity to help more hospitality and accommodation providers in the ways I had hoped.

Over the last decade, I had met hoteliers of smaller establishments at tradeshows and events, noticing how keen they were to improve revenues but didn't know where to begin. On holiday once, the owner of a regional boutique hotel yearned for advice on her distribution set up, asking for my help. I met a pub owner with eight idle hotel rooms at a hospitality conference simply trying to determine if and how to sell them as accommodation. Airbnb owners who wanted assistance maximizing their income and to learn how to generate longer and more robust guest stays – the encounters were endless. During my twenty-year career in hotels I had seen it all—big, small, international, independent, publicly traded or privately owned—and I wanted to help each and every one of them. Finally, I could.

I have always been driven to create a bigger impact, by inspiring and motivating others to achieve their successes, big or small goals, personal or professional, however I possibly could. I am ignited by such a strong desire to share best practices with *everyone*, anyone willing to think outside the box of their current mindset, professional or personal, and consider different methods. This is how *Revenue 20/20: Back to Basics* came about—a book to shine a light of hope and opportunity for improved revenues, complimented by a consulting group of high-quality experts I had the privilege of working with over the years. These all-stars always made my job easier, and I wanted to share them far and wide, particularly with those hotels feeling confused and overwhelmed when most of their business came to a standstill in 2020. At the AHICE conference in Sydney, multiple hoteliers acknowledged that if it hadn't been for guests needing to quarantine in a hotel for fourteen days upon arrival from international flights, they wouldn't have had any business at all. They were indicating that potentially COVID-19 infected people were what had kept their operations afloat… my heart broke for their multi-faceted struggles, and near empty hotels.

With them in mind, I made it my mission to curate the best consultants, coaches, and services, and to offer approachable sessions to hoteliers for a vast range of areas of expertise. Offering their availability more flexibility than traditional consulting companies do means that whatever an operator needs, be it a sounding board for a big decision they need to make or a full outsource of responsibilities, we always have an option for them. I wished to provide a central hub of assistance to every accommodation provider, for situations big and small, that is why Revenue 20/20 was created. Increasing satisfaction, while decreasing stress and confusion—that's what life is all about.

My intention is to share the learnings of my career as far and wide as I possibly can.

> *I'm passionate about seeing people and businesses thrive, not just survive.*

The core components highlighted in each of these chapters are what I have found to be the foundational pillars of a successful business. It's often so easy to get ahead ourselves, inundated and overwhelmed, especially with the seismic shifts that occurred in 2020—the year that changed the way we lived, worked and valued our lives—which is why I believe it is important to bring focus back to the basics. To pivot in a pandemic using the fundamentals that

I've applied to my revenue strategies throughout my career with great results. None of it is earth shattering rocket science, and yet when you get to the last page of this book, my hope is for you to either be energised to apply new ideas to your world with laser focus, or to look back and acknowledge your amazing achievements. Pat yourself on the back if you've been on the right track all along, and if you haven't, that's okay too, it just means this is exactly where you're supposed to be.

20/20—perfect focus and clear vision. Great hindsight for better insights.

Let's check in.

1
FUNDAMENTALS
Transferrable Skills

While the origins of this book stem from hospitality, revenue management principles translate to many industries, especially those with perishable inventory. Any such company generating income is versed in these philosophies. Reading about the fundamentals of this subject may be just what's needed to remind us to focus on what is essential.

Revenue is essential.

Revenue is also personal. We earn a wage or salary that we then spend on life. What's leftover is profit. Top line revenue, bottom line profit. Costs are a different topic altogether and vary greatly by many factors. Revenue, however, is universal. We're all here to gather more dollars, be it for ourselves, our business, our team or organization. Revenue is something we can all agree we want to maximize for our pre-determined cause.

Economic Trends & Cycles

It's worth noting that nearly every sector cycles through trends, highs and lows, and that many global economic fluctuations are factors of revenue. For example, the cinema business tends to cycle every three years between a 'beyond-Blockbuster' hit (is it even appropriate to reference it as a blockbuster anymore? I digress...) and a few years of treading water through low revenue-generating films. COVID-19 has certainly flipped cinemas on their heads. Delays in film releases has bucked typical cinema trends right off the bull. In fashion, cycles and recycles are a common occurrence. They happen in precise moments, usually every fifteen years and always in different ways, but nonetheless inspired by a particular era that came before.

However, let's assume you already know that about your particular field. There are hotels in New Zealand who have correlated hotel room rates to the price per litre of milk! Revenue optimisation is not exempt to economic recessions or depressions, but as with many industries, there are often many creative ways to keep the lights on. Room and occupancy rates in hotels fluctuate more noticeably in the five-star luxury sectors, as spend will tighten when consumer confidence wanes. It's also this class of hotels that have the most leverage when it comes to pricing, because their operating costs tend to be relatively similar to most other hotels, yet they have a broader spectrum of price range to play with. They can mitigate profit losses during economic downturns if they pivot accordingly.

Perishable Inventory

Perish *(verb) to become destroyed or ruined: cease to exist.*[i]
Perishable *(adjective)*
1 (especially of food) likely to decay or go bad quickly.
1.1 (of something abstract) having a brief life or significance; transitory.[ii]

Food is often our first thought when we hear the term 'perishable inventory', particularly produce (things that can go bad quickly), yet many industries have products with a shorter shelf life than fruit. Products that are time dependent are by far the most difficult to sell optimally and to manage availability for. The inventory in hospitality, be it guestrooms or restaurant tables, is highly perishable. If you don't sell it for 'time', then that time and money is gone. You snooze on your opportunity, you lose the chance to sell.

> *Price too high and you won't sell anything.*
> *Price too low and you won't have enough to sell.*
> *There's not one right answer.*

The most common examples of perishable inventory are hotel rooms, rental space of any kind, airplane seats, rental cars and movie, concert or event tickets. Some of these examples have the advantage of flexibility. For example, a cinema can cancel a show if no tickets sell, rental cars can be sent to another location with higher demand, and an airline can add or remove flights during peak or off-peak periods. Hotels, however, can't build more rooms for New Year's Eve and then pack them away over low season. It's much harder for hotels to shut down their operations during slow times without jeopardizing future business, and bleeding ongoing costs without any income.

I love the idea of transportable hotel pods, or a fleet of Airstream Caravans that can be sent over to hotels for highly constrained dates, allowing them to continue to sell over sold-out events. Trailer or caravan parks are probably the closest there is to this concept, although Airbnb owners seem to be picking up on high demand trends too.

> *Knowing how much you have in supply, and how many are expected to demand it, are the core principles of revenue management.*

So… What is Revenue Management?

Revenue Management *the application of disciplined analytics that predict consumer behaviour at the micro-market levels and optimize product availability and price to maximize revenue growth.*

The primary aim of revenue management is selling the right product to the right customer, at the right time, for the right price and with the right pack. The essence of this discipline is in understanding customers' perception of product value and accurately aligning product prices, placement and availability with each customer segment.[iii]

Seemingly complex, and yet very straightforward.

> We're trying to sell the right product (supply) to the right customer (demand) at the right time (when they are ready and willing to pay).

Where Did Revenue Management Come From?

The first formal introduction of pricing based on demand, at least for the travel industry, was by a British airline employee, Ken Littlewood, in 1972. 'Littlewood's Rule' was the first form of yield management for aviation, and not long after, replicated by hotels to 'revenue manage' their rooms. 'Yield' and 'Revenue' have been used interchangeably by these industries, however today they focus on essentially the same thing—maximising money coming in. Here's a textbook definition for comparison, you'll notice that yield management is more in line with the multi-disciplinary aspect of what Revenue Managers do:

Yield Management: *A set of yield maximization strategies and tactics to improve the profitability of certain businesses. It's complex because it involves several aspects of management control, including rate management, revenue streams management, and distribution channel management.*

Yield management is multidisciplinary because it blends elements of marketing, operations, and financial management into a highly successful new approach. Yield management strategists must frequently work with one or more other departments when designing and implementing yield management strategies.[iv]

Who is a Revenue Manager?

This is a great question, with no clear-cut answer, because a Revenue Manager is many things. In the past, the explanation of what a Revenue Manager (or RM for short) does, was to liken them to an analyst or data scientist (someone who interprets the numbers and then adjusts pricing accordingly). But the realm of RMs extends far beyond that today. Anything that generates revenue, and particularly when selling perishable products, from pool cabanas to seats in a restaurant, has the potential to be impacted by an RM's talents. Unfortunately, as an industry we're not really 'there' yet, not universally at least. However, we are evolving at a decent pace thanks to software and technology becoming more advanced, easily accessible, and affordable.

> *In today's world, RMs need to be more than number crunchers. They need to have a solid commercial understanding of the business and be effective communicators.*

They encompass all elements of yield management. Though their role is continuously evolving and expanding, one thing is certain: Where there's money to be made, there's a role for revenue management.

Art vs. Science

If you've heard any industry talks about the subject, you'd recall revenue management being affectionately described as 'a balance between art and science'. That's accurate to a degree, but also not entirely true…

Is it art, or is it science? Do you *feel* a price and go in that direction? Or do you trust the black and white of science and sell in a way that has been proven historically by data?

> You do both. But it's not a 'balance'.

Balance sounds like a child's desire for 'even Steven' (if you get one then I get one, which makes it perfectly fair). That suggests if I spend x hours on work, then I should spend x hours on life. Raise your hand now if that's how it works in your world! The reality is that work is life and life is work, whether you love it or hate it. Balancing sounds like I'm riding on a wagon. I could be sitting on the seat, or hanging off the side of it, held on only by a rope caught around my leg. Technically I'm on the wagon, but dangling by a limb, not exactly 'balance'. That's no way to live, or to operate a business.

I could go on and on about the word itself and how we need to dispel balance and many other words from our vocabulary. Did you 'lose' weight, or did you burn it off with sweat, pain and tears? If you really woke up one day and couldn't find the weight you once had, please tell me how. Did you 'find' time for that project, or did you chisel and carve it out of your daily grind to focus on it as a priority? Again, if I could 'find time' in say my pocket or my wallet, my life would look vastly different right now. I digress…

Okay, so you get that it's not 'balance', but what is it?

Integration

You're not balancing on a beam—you're incorporating different aspects of your world into one world in the most productive way you know how. And that's exactly what you do with revenue management. You've seen the movies where robots take over, then the whole world is saved when human emotions (faith, love or whatever) come into play again. The automated robotics of it would be an RM world based solely on science. In contrast, movies with carefree characters who are entirely free-spirited and unaware, don't conform to the rest of the world, and stereotypically don't usually triumph or live awfully long, would be a system based only on the art.

Someone said recently on an industry panel, "It's not 'art' anymore, it's 'judgment.'" Call it what you like, some people like bad art and some people have poor judgment, I'm not here to split hairs. The point is, you need to be looking forward *and* looking back. You need gut instinct with hard data. You need to see the odds stacked against the lead character, but support them anyway as they forge ahead, and then everyone lives happily ever after because he/she tried something extraordinary.

'Integration' was derived from 'Integrato', the Latin root 'to make whole', and that's exactly what we're all trying to do—incorporate all the moving parts of life/business to make one that's whole. To put it into an equation:

$$\text{Art (service, value)} + \text{Science (price, analytics)} = \text{Integration (optimal revenue).}$$

It's trial and error, push and pull, yin and yang, balance and integration. There's no black and white or wrong and right. It's simple, but it's not easy.

It's life.

2
COMMUNICATION
Words Over Numbers?

I know you were expecting to see analytics as the forefront chapter of a revenue book, but times have changed. Make no mistake, numbers are the very backbone of revenue's existence and abundance, however there's also a limit to their use.

These days, we want more out of life in general. Analytics are more freely available in our personal lives—banks tell us where we're spending, apps can categorize it down to the morning coffee if we so choose. Social media platforms count the number of 'likes' we accrue for every thought we share publicly, phones count the number of calls made and for how long, and the time we spend on screens. Airlines track our travel miles, grocery stores how many dollars, while loyalty clubs for literally everything we purchase tell us how many points we've earned—you get where I'm going.

Our lives are full of numbers.

But what does it all tell us? What life-improving action can we take from all this data? Of course, there's plenty we can do with it, reduce life's stressors is a big one. We can create realistic budgets for ourselves, track our spending, and find ways to increase income and reduce costs (all in a day's work for revenue and finance managers). But the rest? What is essential?

And this is my (very wordy) point. We'll discuss later the epidemic of over analysing, but for now, let's emphasize the message:

Focus on That Which is Essential

A few years ago, I read a book by Greg McKeown, *Essentialism – The Disciplined Pursuit of Less*. I immediately gave a copy to my boss at the time. Don't misunderstand, said leader was amazing. I still have the highest level of respect and admiration for him (not everyone can say that about the people they've worked for, I know), but it's easy for even the most well intended individuals to get carried away with reports and documenting from time to time. I believe we *all* need a reminder of where to set, or reset, our boundaries to occasionally. What boundaries, in this case with numbers, do we allow within our critical thinking and decision-making realm, and what do we let fall outside these borders, classifying them simply as 'too much information'? This will vary by day, week, month, even minute, however it's important to always keep essentialism in your frame of mind, to stay focused on key objectives instead of running away with the number fairies.

McKeown's book is worth reading no matter who you are or what you do, but particularly for managers with multiple teams, tasks or revenue generating priorities. I've met many an analytical RM in my time, but rarely does one cross my team with the same expertise in communication skills. Hands down, the best RMs I've worked with have had a high-level understanding of communication and can articulate their points in a succinct manner that's been well thought out for the audience they're presenting to. I think it's safe to say that the best leaders in general possess this skill as well.

I'll highlight just two essential (pun intended) points from McKeown's book. (Note: If you've ever felt overwhelmed, even slightly, at any point in your life, I highly recommend you read it in its entirety). Basically, the author's points are this—take a life of tangled scribble and reshape it into something more manageable:[v]

The Model

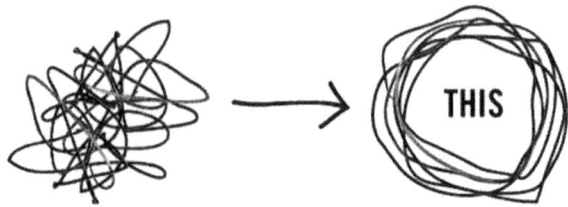

	Nonessentialist	Essentialist
Thinks	**ALL THINGS TO ALL PEOPLE** "I have to." "It's all important." "How can I fit it all in?"	**LESS BUT BETTER** "I choose to." "Only a few things really matter." "What are the trade-offs?"
Does	**THE UNDISCIPLINED PURSUIT OF MORE** Reacts to what's most pressing Says "yes" to people without really thinking Tries to force execution at the last moment	**THE DISCIPLINED PURSUIT OF LESS** Pauses to discern what really matters Says "no" to everything except the essential Removes obstacles to make execution easy
Gets	**LIVES A LIFE THAT DOES NOT SATISFY** Takes on too much, and work suffers Feels out of control Is unsure of whether the right things got done Feels overwhelmed and exhausted	**LIVES A LIFE THAT REALLY MATTERS** Chooses carefully in order to do great work Feels in control Gets the right things done Experiences joy in the journey

And when it comes to leadership, focus on just seven characteristics, ones we all should strive to possess:[vi]

	Non-Essentialist	Essentialist
MIND-SET	Everything to everyone	Less but better
TALENT	Hires people frantically and creates a "Bozo explosion."	Ridiculously selective on talent and removes people who hold the team back.
STRATEGY	Pursues a straddled strategy where everything is a priority.	Defines an essential intent by answering the question, "If we could only do one thing, what would it be?" Eliminates the non-essential distractions.
EMPOWERMENT	Allows ambiguity over who is doing what. Decisions are capricious.	Focuses on each team member's highest role and goal of contribution.
COMMUNICATION	Talks in code.	Listens to get to what is essential.
ACCOUNTABILITY	Checks in too much or is so busy he or she checks out altogether. Sometimes does both: disrupting the focus of the group and then being absent to the group.	Checks in with people in a gentle way to see how he or she can remove obstacles and enable small wins.
RESULT	A fractured team that makes a millimetre of progress in a million directions	A unified team that breaks through to the next level of contribution

It's such a worthwhile investment to read this book and all of McKeown's work, including his latest release, 'Effortless – Make It Easier to Do What Matters Most'.

Know Your Audience (and when to shut up)

Let's be honest, money/finance/revenue—it's an important subject, but it's a bit dry. Capturing the attention of your audience, keeping them interested and convincing them to buy into your proposal is not always easy, particularly if they aren't 'numbers people'. It's important to clarify your objective and get straight to the point, providing just enough evidence to support your request, but not so much that you lose them. Knowing your audience is not only key, but also critical to your business's success. The universal law of 'less is more' is crucial to any conversation—particularly with revenue and analytics. No one likes a rambler.

In Writing

Writing relates to presentations, strategic documents, emails, posts, memos, footnotes, reports—you name it. A lot of people write like they speak (I might be one of them) but knowing when to shut up is just as significant as knowing what to share. I've seen, and written, many an email that are as long as a novel, thankfully I've changed my ways.

Sharing all your thoughts can make you feel justified, righteous, and all important while writing it, however the receiver isn't usually as enthused. Most who receive an email like that get overwhelmed, their eyes glaze over as they scan for key words or sentences that might be relevant to them as a recipient. Others may feel inundated by information overload and move onto the next email, promising themselves to go back and read it later.

> *Don't lose your audience like that. Their time is as valuable as yours, so don't waste either.*

A turning point for me came when I attended training on effective communication. I'd highly recommend you get a comms refresh in a course like this, no matter who you are or what you do. Here are a few takeaways that have saved many minutes of mental load and memory for my email recipients:

Your subject line should tell the recipient exactly what you need. For example:
    Subject: For your approval—a few words of what you want approved.

The body should have one-line paragraphs, and one-sentence bullet points whenever possible. Such as:
    Objective: A quick recap sentence as a refresher.
    Background: Research or information about the subject using bullet points.
    To Action: A sentence or bullet points with your request for the recipient.

For example:

Hi Norman,

We've discussed offering incentives to our front desk agents for upselling Executive rooms.

Background:
- 60% of guests staying in Executive rooms last month were comp upgrades upon check-in.
- A $20 average nightly upgrade charge would have resulted in incremental revenue of $40k.

For your approval:
- Incentivise the agents with a 10% commission on total upsell revenue they generate.
- Trial for 60 days, review results with yourself and Front Office Manager, discuss next steps.

Please let me know if approved and I will create the framework, logistics, and rollout for the team.

Kind regards,

Kristin
Revenue Manager

If you really need (or want) to get wordy, attach it to your email. That way recipients can review it when they're ready to digest it. Keeping the email itself to high-level, short and sweet bullet points means it will get read, while anything longer increases the odds of it being overlooked.

In Print

This also applies to your presentations, standard operating procedures, memos, marketing, packages and promotions. The less wordy and complicated, the better. If they have questions, they'll ask. If they need more detail, you'll hear about it. And if you hear about it enough, you can decide if more information needs to be communicated.

Cut the Fluff

Chances are you already know this, but lose the non-essential words. Write how you write, whatever it is, and just before hitting send or print, save it, re-read your words, and remove the unimportant.

Here's an example:
- As most of you are aware, we've decided to implement a program that will offer incentives to our front desk team when they are able to upsell a guest into an Executive room.

Instead try:
- We'll be offering incentives to front desk agents for upsells to Executive rooms.

Much better.

In Person

Meetings and presentations will be a part of any revenue person's role. While stereotypically RM's tend to be introverts and analytical, the way we present ourselves and our opinions is unquestionably important. If you don't have confidence in your ability and beliefs, your message won't be given the respect and credibility it deserves. You don't have to hire the politician, yet the person you choose to look after your money—how they present themselves, their numbers, and *your business*—is critical. Don't dismiss the numbers people as ones who won't need to possess good communication skills. Yes, they can be very black and white, it's numbers after all, but they should also have a decent understanding of who they're speaking to and how that audience best digests information. Which leads us to…

If you Don't Know, THEN ASK

Some people love a good spreadsheet, the more numbers the better. Others want you to *talk* them through the plan. And there are those who like a visual layout of maps, graphs and charts instead of numbers. How do you figure out who likes what? In some cases, you'll come to understand their preference through a few initial interactions. Are they asking you to *describe* the reports you've brought with you, or do they light up when you show them a visual representation of your competitors on a geographical map? Or both?

When you aren't sure, just ask. I wouldn't have known for sure a CEO I worked for was a visual person had her Executive Assistant not confirmed it with me one day. You're far better off getting clarity than making assumptions and creating extra work for yourself. Knowing what people prefer doesn't mean you need to change every number into an infographic or a graph into a chart. Some things won't be able to transpose, and that's okay. A detailed pricing report will never be able to be anything but a spreadsheet full of numbers, but a competitive analysis may be able to be represented with logos and graphics instead of letters and numbers. Knowing how your audience prefers to communicate and comprehend information is critical to getting your message across, and interpreted as you intended.

The Objective of Meetings

When I first read *The 4-Hour Work Week* by Timothy Ferriss,[vii] I was sceptical about how anyone could reduce forty hours into four, and I still am. However, I do understand his premise, which was a big reason I started outsourcing some of my tasks and work projects to consultants. There were some real gems of advice that we can all apply, such as not having meetings just to have meetings. They're usually the ones you dread going to, find yourself thinking of ways not to attend, and loathe being in. I used to get such anxiety sitting in meetings I didn't need to be in, especially when my time could be better spent on my team's priorities and goals.

Stop. Don't meet to meet. If your meeting doesn't have a clear objective that defines what will be accomplished *in that meeting*, don't bother having one. But there's a fine line between being a team player and looking like you're 'too good' to go to something, don't be that person either. Communicate your opinion to the team involved and brainstorm more mutually productive ways to align your objectives. Saving time for your team saves energy, and money too. Sometimes these meetings would be better served with a quick group email or conference call, or by recurring fortnightly instead of weekly. Don't be afraid to talk it out with everyone else. Being honest is more beneficial than bringing low energy and a reluctant attitude to your meeting.

Communication summary in one sentence:

> *Focus on what's essential, be upfront about your intention, clear and concise in your delivery, and you can't go wrong.*

3
ANALYTICS

The Importance of Numbers

Following the chapter on concise and effective communication, the importance of numbers can be summed up as this:

Numbers are what we're all here for. A business cannot exist or operate without them. They're most important. Period.

Daily Habits

> *"The upside of habits is we can do things without thinking. The downside is that we stop paying attention to little errors."*[viii]
> James Clear
> *Atomic Habits*

Another book I'd highly recommend is James Clear's *Atomic Habits*. He highlights the importance of good practices and layering little ones on top of each other to create a big impact. However, he also warns about getting too comfortable in them, leading to complacency and carelessness. He urges us to check in regularly with our habits to ensure they're still serving us and emphasises how they also need deliberate practice to ensure ultimate success or mastery of a skill.

Complacency can happen so easily when working with numbers without a deliberate practice in place. You look at your pick-up report, or the spreadsheet showing what bookings (or purchases) have been made each day, next to rows of prices for your product and those of your competitors. Dates, rates and occupancy percentages are numbers upon numbers on a page. If your mind isn't right because you are not focused, your revenue management decisions won't be either.

Revenue managers find ways to highlight outliers, building formulas into spreadsheets to colour cells in bold hues when certain anomalies occur. The alarming numbers stand out so you really pay attention to them. Yes, the ability to seemingly subconsciously adjust prices on a pick-up report, without blinking, can feel magical. Even so, every good RM needs the help of a second (or third, or fourth) set of eyes, because sometime the numbers all start to look the same. My best advice, in life and in pricing, is:

Be present.

Do I have your attention again, or have you started skimming the pages to simply get through this book? Presence is paramount. I know it, you know it, but it's often easier said than done, particularly in hospitality. Numbers are the last thing that scream for your attention in the hotel world.

A guest complaint, a group pricing quote, a wholesale travel agent requesting an increase on their allotment (don't be scared, we'll get to all these in a later chapter) *those* will command your attention first. Your boss, your staff, unanswered emails, the missed call and the to-do list will cry and whine for your response—but that forecast report, the pricing spreadsheet, the promotion analysis—they won't make a peep. Does that make them any less important?

NO! You know it, I know it.

But sometimes they become the neglected task if you don't build a routine of tackling them consistently each day. Remember the saying, '80% of the output comes from 20% of the work'? Universal, particularly for revenue. Obviously as a manager, employees still need your help and please don't ignore that guest, group, sales lead, etc. Just remember to make time for your critical 20% workload with a religious commitment. Write down when, where and how often you'll do it, then put it on your calendar.

The most successful RMs I know have steadfast routines that barely alter. Most people around them are aware too, so they know not to disturb or request time with them over these periods. Making big financial decisions, such as pricing and forecasting, requires deep focus and concentration—they may look like mere dollars and percentage points, but to paraphrase Clear's wisdom:

> Don't miss the small stuff, the tiny improvements, while you're chasing the big moments. Those small things, in the long term, can be what makes the big difference.

As Clear says:

> *"If you can get 1% better each day for 1 year, you'll end up 37 times better by the time you're done."*

Lastly, he references a plane's flight path when he writes, "A very small shift in direction can lead to a very meaningful change in destination. Similarly, a slight change in daily habits can guide your life to a different destination."

Good daily habits, yours and your team's, are critical to the success of revenue management.

Analysis Paralysis

Have you ever gotten lost in cyber space? Gone astray in the World Wide Web? It starts with something innocent, like searching for Excel formulas on Google, which takes you to a website about Excel. That website suggests you enrol in their 'Excel for hotel managers' course, which of course you start to consider. As you read the details however, you notice a banner ad from a competitor hotel on the right side of the screen. You begin to wonder what it's about, because depending on how sharp the offer is, it could give you an idea of their occupancy holdings. High price, high expected demand. Low price, they're desperate to get business on the books. Turns out the ad featuring your competitor hotel is actually for a group buying site, a Luxury Escapes for example. They have more than just your neighbouring hotel, but also extremely discounted fares for flights to Bali. 'Should I go to Bali?' you ask yourself, as you click on the offer. The next thing you know it has been an hour, and you are no closer to finishing your excel formula than you are to taking a holiday in Bali.

This is the quintessential meaning of 'analysis paralysis'. Start with a good intention, but end with a side-track distraction so big it takes over the original pursuit! For RMs, this is most often caused by the tantalizing torture of too much data. Start with a simple query, such as why last night's Average Daily Rate (ADR) was low, and end with an eagerness to understand if your prices ending in 9s instead of 5s had *everything* to do with the lower ADR of your Tuesdays in December.

Analysis is not a bad thing, we know that, but analysis *paralysis* is, because it's exactly that—*paralysing*. It distracts you from the essential understanding by tempting you with a 'beautiful mind' moment. Convincing yourself if you dig deep enough into the numbers, they will surely reveal that the answer is possibly, maybe, probably, hypothetically related to that one you think you thought of that might, maybe, surely identify the probability of the reason that answers your question.

Do you see where I'm going? Too much of *anything* is too much. The grass is always greener on the other side, and this means each hotel must be content with the greenery *they* are able to grow or influence. Over analysing elements that are anomalies or largely out of your control isn't time well spent. It doesn't mean hotels shouldn't benchmark against other properties or understand their points of difference compared to the competitors, they should, and their grass may very well be greener. However, as it relates to the data measures within a hotel itself, everything in moderation is key. This applies to revenue strategies as well; too much occupancy and someone more senior will suggest that focusing on higher rate would have been better, hindsight being 20/20 of course. Too high a rate and someone else might toss the old saying, "heads in beds is the name of the game—sacrifice rate," into the conversation.

You can't win. But you *can* back up your decisions with numbers. Let the data *assist* you, not *overtake* you. Numbers are a manager's best friend, but boundaries need to exist. Just as no one likes the needy friend (the one who doesn't know when to shut up and listen), that's what over analysis can be to a business if they lose sight of what is essential.

Healthy Boundaries

The first crucial step to setting limits to the science is communicating objectives and desired outcomes to your analysts. Desired outcomes might sound like I'm implying data should be falsified or manipulated—definitely not. However, if we're being honest, the numbers can say anything we want them to, depending on how we massage them or what we put emphasis on or choose to show. For example, I could analyse and conclude that last night's low ADR was because it rained, and that every time it has rained recently the rate has been lower than last year. Is that helpful? In a resort property maybe. Is it preventable? No. Can you action a plan around those findings? Again, as a strategic 'rainy season' plan, sure, but as a 'Tuesday night tactic only if it's raining', probably not. What was the point of understanding weather and ADR correlation in the first place if we don't have any levers to pull once we do?

Communicating outcomes and objectives is the first step to a healthy relationship with data.

The second is brainstorming a few broad, high-level hypotheses of what the reasons, obstacles or opportunities might be to give direction. Numbers do provide black and white findings, so we want a yes/no, true/false, do it/abandon outcome from the analysis. It doesn't mean we need to do everything the science says, or even believe the results for that matter. If something doesn't look right, ask someone to double check the numbers or run the report again. An error in a calculation, or accidentally using partial data instead of the complete results, is not unheard of. Mistakes can happen, trust your gut, question the accuracy. Once you're satisfied the findings are correct, you have a solid platform to make your best decisions from.

Here's the kicker though—no one actually knows, and no one ever truly will, because each human's recollection of the same event in the past will differ based on their perception, beliefs and opinion. We will never know how things would have turned out differently because time is never replicated. Days can be similar but never identical, there are no do-overs, just trial and error, trying and reviewing. Nothing is certain, nothing is guaranteed; it's the blessing and the curse in life. Being able to accept change, to know when to go with the flow or when to embrace a shift in direction, is what will keep you nimble. Maintaining an open mind offers the best chance of being able to pivot in a pandemic. Analytics are only one piece of the puzzle of historical understanding, so they will never paint the full picture.

The most capable managers know that as with almost anything in life, revenue management requires a balanced approach of integration—science and art, words and numbers, analysing, and accepting that there are always extenuating circumstances beyond what we already know. They know that their work is about progress, and that progress, not perfection, is enough to base good decisions on.

Science vs. Art

Businesses that only look at data are missing an opportunity to understand their customers, play on their emotional needs and maximize revenue. Owners who only look at the 'art' of how they price their products are losing key insights into how and why people are buying from them. An 'art' priced hotel might do seasonal rates, January to June are always $200 dollars and July to December are always $400, no ifs, ands or buts. Easy, yes. Profitable, sure. Maximum revenue potential, not so great. In contrast, a 'science' driven hotel might look only at the numbers—what are their competitors selling at, how many rooms have they sold, are they holding more reservations or less than this time last year, and at a higher or lower rate? This approach is solid, however if they fail to factor the flight halting thunderstorm outside, or that their closest competitor is literally in flames (extreme, I know) then they too are missing potential pitfalls or opportunities.

Companies who understand the integration of art and science are arguably the most successful.

Here are two real life examples from my career. When I was Director of Revenue at The Westin Hotel in Las Vegas, I was always in close communication with the Director of Sales and we had a healthy working relationship. The Director of Sales was a gun, she played to win and was exceptionally good at what she did. She was balanced in her sales approach with clients, making them feel their needs were seen and understood, while feeling happy with our terms and pricing and their decision to choose us. Having these skills is an amazing talent.

One day I got a call from her, "Kristin, you're going to love me. I just secured a piece of business for next month—twenty rooms for $329 a night!"

I checked the dates and the prices we were selling online and paused.

"That's great, Sandra," I replied, "but we're only selling $200 a night over those dates."

"Oh, I know," she said, "but the client's budget was $400, so I offered them less than what they expected, and they're thrilled to be staying with us! Win, win! Besides, you can just take up the prices online."

I know what you're thinking, she got us more ADR than I was getting elsewhere which is great—she accomplished an amazing feat by increasing our average rate with a group locked in at a high price. But... she failed to recognize that as RM, I would not be able to justify taking up our public pricing for the remaining 300 rooms we had left to sell simply because she'd locked in twenty at an incredible price. Selling rooms at $339 online (slightly higher than $329 to 'protect' the group rate) would price me well above all my competitors. Travellers would likely choose them over us, so it didn't make sense. Her 'artistic' ability to sell ice to Eskimos wasn't doing us any favours in that instance.

Yes, Sandra is smart. And Sandra is a leader in hotel sales. Sandra could read people and somehow make them happy to be paying more! It's a gift. However, this time her skill came at the cost of 'room revenue logic'. I'm not discrediting her effort, and I'll explain why after this next example.

In contrast, I later worked for Caesars Entertainment group and looked after room revenue, primarily for the Flamingo Hotel. To give it context, the luxurious namesake, Caesars Palace, was right across the street from the Flamingo, with Harrah's and Imperial Palace just next door (although both not so luxurious, nor nearly as nice as the Flamingo or Caesars back then).

The 'bread and butter' of cash paying room revenue in Las Vegas is from big conferences and city-wide conventions. Global and national tradeshows, conventions and associations would contract hundreds of rooms per night for many consecutive nights, at multiple hotels, in order to accommodate all their anticipated attendees. However, as none of us had crystal balls, meeting planners of these city-wide events included, these large blocks of rooms wouldn't materialize exactly as planned. Perhaps more would book to stay at one hotel, less at another. Or there would be less attendance overall because of economic impacts on that industry at the time, or an overzealous expectation of participants. A myriad of factors. This meant that the key to maximizing revenues over these dates was to forecast *each* group's potential pickup, at each hotel, then *oversell* the remaining available rooms accordingly. Forecasting each group was determined by client or meeting planner insights on registration so far, pace rooms booked compared to last year's event so far, as well as reviewing group pickup numbers in each hotel's PMS and comparing them with other properties in your company.

There is always risk to this 'oversell' approach, but more often than not, with big groups and citywide events there are high 'wash' factors. For hotels, a 'wash' is the percentage comparison of the number of rooms contracted versus the number that actualised or showed up. Understanding historical wash of a particular repeat group, or averages of those with similar booking styles that had recently stayed, gives hotels the ability to forecast future turnout more accurately. If a revenue manager didn't wash the group blocks enough, their hotel would be left with a large number of rooms released to sell, possibly just a few weeks away from arrival. Similar to the Westin's example, the public selling pricing for all these unexpected rooms remaining would need to be extremely high to protect the large group rates, and the large number of rooms booked at that rate, to 'protect' the contracted block.

In one such instance, let's say it was the Consumer Electronic Show (CES), one of the largest and most lucrative citywide conventions. Our hotels within the Caesar's Entertainment group were receiving lots of block requests at solid rates, so much so that each had started to decline them due to capacity. I started to think big picture... for the hotel group, not just my property (something I encourage *every* hotel who is part of a group or affiliation to do). Caesar's Palace had recently received a group cancellation, resulting in an unexpectedly high number of rooms to sell. Dropping their online rate wasn't feasible as it posed the risk of undercutting the group rates they already had contracted. So, I decided I would purposely oversell The Flamingo and 'walk' (or relocate) surplus guests over to Caesar's to stay instead. Win, win.

Now if you work in a hotel, or have ever simply stayed in one, you know that relocating guests, or being relocated, is not easy or fun. The guest is inconvenienced, and they expect compensation, and they don't want to go—unless of course you explain that they've been upgraded. Everyone likes an upgrade! Would you object to being bumped up to business class from economy on a flight? I wouldn't! Relocating guests is almost a pleasure when it involves a nicer product, there's mutual gratitude.

In the end, we relocated more than 100 bookings to Caesars Palace (the rest of the rooms washed or cancelled as anticipated) and our group's Vice President of Revenue at the time was impressed. He wanted more of this tactic applied whenever one hotel had high demand and the other had high need. It's a great idea in theory, but realistically it's only easily executed when you go from low to high quality, not any other way. From a 'scientific' point of view, he expected The Flamingo could relocate to Harrah's and Harrah's to Imperial Palace (each were a downgrade at the time.) That was a hard sell. As a guest, I'd expect compensation, "I paid for Premium class, and you're trying to put me in economy? I don't think so, not without a refund."

Again, if you think I'm discrediting his intelligence or skill (of which he had both) I'm not. Our Vice President at that time was strictly a numbers man. His background was in the science of analytics, not in hospitality. He liked that we shifted revenue numbers from one property to another, but he didn't fully understand the confrontational guest service aspect of forcing someone to stay where they didn't choose. There was also the added repercussion of customer dissatisfaction to consider, and how far that could spread, affecting future guests. In Las Vegas, a city of hotels where competition is on your doorstep *and* backyard, it was an extremely critical factor.

To conclude, the point of these two stories is not to highlight any human faults, in fact the executives were very skilled and experienced. Rather, it's to showcase two examples of where sole focus on either the 'art' or 'science' of pricing can be financially detrimental. However, they also emphasize that nothing is black and white. In the case of the group paying $329 at The Westin, we upgraded their twenty attendees to deluxe rooms and threw in a few amenities to add value and maintain their contracted rate while pricing slightly below it online. Sandra also secured a few smaller groups in the $200s, which not only helped fill the hotel, but also gave her clients a satisfied sense of getting a great offer, paying well less than the higher public rate we had available.

At the Flamingo, our relocations evolved to be more forward thinking. We identified ideal candidates to walk and called them in advance to offer an upgraded room type at a lesser hotel. If they agreed, great, we'd transfer the booking to the other property. If they didn't, we would make a note in their reservation not to relocate them, even upon arrival, and called the next guest. We still had time to ask the remaining guests on our list. It was the integration of analytics and emotional intelligence that always would make the most sense and money. However, it was just as critical to accurately forecast each upcoming group using historical trends, data and future attendee insights in order to maximise revenue.

Reducing public pricing lower than what has already booked, particularly last minute, is detrimental in many ways. It upsets the client or meeting planner, who inevitably starts receiving complaints from attendees, or notices themselves that there are lower rates available than what they were contracted. It also opens the possibility of the hotel honouring the lower public rate for their attendees who were already reserved, leading to an unexpected reduction in forecasted revenue. Fundamentally, it also dissuades travellers from booking in advance. If they experience the reality of cheaper rates being available last minute, their booking habits start to shift that way too, as we've seen in recent years. With groups, the more accurate the adjustment made to each block of rooms is, reflecting the forecasted attendance as far in advance as possible, the better the opportunity for other market segments to fill the void.

This is particularly prevalent for the casino hotels because high-value players are more beneficial to a property's *total* revenue than the average last minute online booking would be.

Incremental Revenue

What is incremental or ancillary revenue? I use both terms interchangeably, but put simply, it's any extra money that comes in from means other than the original or main purchase. In retail, that might mean someone who buys a new phone (primary revenue) also buys a phone case and earphones (incremental). In hotels, it could mean the person staying and paying for overnight accommodation (primary revenue) also orders room service and a spa treatment (ancillary).

This is important to think about and is the direction revenue management is evolving towards. The casinos already apply this method, and so do cruise lines. Get people in, even at low prices, and statistically they will spend the money they saved on their reservation in your outlets once on site. Many resorts have this benefit too, but unfortunately most hotels within proximity to anything interesting don't. As an industry we could all improve on strategically analysing ways to increase incremental revenue.

Achieving the maximum ancillary or incremental income for a business's 'secondary' revenue generating outlets is about understanding the 'big picture' of what a guest brings to your business, not just their room and tax charge. Having a software or tool that can retrieve the ancillary analytics from your property management system not only provides a better understanding of all that extra spend, it helps you create better offers and promotions to bring in more money to the whole establishment, not just rooms. It also allows us to think big picture—do we need to sacrifice a little bit of room rate, knowing that once they're in our hotel they'll spend more on site? Maybe.

This is exactly what the casino industry has mastered. They can see, on average, how much money their players spend each day in their casino. They calculate this daily worth and apply it towards discounted offers on accommodation to entice those guests to come visit more frequently.

As a hypothetical example, a player spends $50 at the blackjack table every time he visits his favourite casino hotel in Las Vegas. That is good, although not a monumental amount for a casino, so they might send him promotions with room offers that are roughly $50 less than the public price. Interestingly, many players may not even be aware of how much they gamble, in total, or per visit, so $50 off could seem generous to this person. He feels rewarded and motivated to visit, the hotel gets room revenue, and the casino gets gaming revenue, not to mention what he might spend on food, drinks and entertainment. It's an overall revenue win for the business. Similarly, if a high-roller player averages a casino spend of $1,000 or $10,000 a day, he'd likely be enticed with much more, say a free room or spacious suite plus many more perks such as show tickets, dining etc. A great value and enticement for the guest, and relatively low costs for the hotel.

I encourage all businesses to brainstorm ways in which they can entice their guests using little to no cost amenities that add value to the customer. Even vouchers for a free drink or discount can convince a person to spend at a place they may not have chosen otherwise. This is best ascertained by drilling down into the numbers to see who spends what and where.

How do I do that?

"Wait, what?" you're thinking, "we don't have that kind of system or way to look at that, what are businesses like ours supposed to do?"

The answer is simple—Revenue Management Software Systems (or RMS), competitive benchmarking reports, and *outsourcing*.

Revenue Management Software

Revenue Management Software (RMS) systems are rapidly becoming more hotel friendly, plug-and-play, easy to use options for properties wanting more accurate analytics with less human intervention. Decades ago, at the beginning of my career, RMS systems were big and clunky. They were extremely expensive and very intricate, and users needed a lot of training, time and concentration to operate them at a level that would see them perform well *and* actually benefit the hotel. Back then, they needed to latch onto your Property Management System (PMS) or point of sale (POS) transaction software, and then stay latched on like an octopus with tentacles, suctioned in and around every IT element you owned. I lost count of the number of times in my night audit years that I accessed the forbidden IT hardware room to reboot all systems when they stopped syncing with each other in the middle of the night. Moments of panic for the overnight team, waiting, and then a technical resuscitation! System interfaces back then weren't easy or fun, but they were beneficial.

The good news is that systems today aren't so rigid anymore. Most are web based, and many have an app version for quick stat checks from your phone. Some are basic, simple, 'lite' and perfect for independent, rural or simple strategy hotels. In some cases, you can get key revenue analytics simply by sending the RMS provider a few of your PMS reports via email each day. Even better, hotel systems can usually schedule these reports to generate and send automatically, which is ideal. The RMS, in turn, digests the data it receives and instantly produces useful dashboards that display metrics such as revenue, demand, insights of booking trends aggregated over time, and much more.

For larger hotels, chains or more complex hotels, the bigger, more robust systems in the market might be better suited. They do usually require more finessing, set up, and regular attention, however this ensures a higher accuracy in producing more relevant pricing suggestions and revenue forecasts, which makes the time and effort spent maintaining them worthwhile.

Regardless of the RMS brand, I liken all of them to big (expensive) scientific calculators—they do a lot of the number crunching for you; however they still need someone to push the buttons. That is to say that while RMS systems have come a long way to be more 'plug and play' and suit all types of businesses, they are not a replacement for the Revenue Manager or person you have fulfilling these duties. Instead, they are a 'tool' in your arsenal that can help improve your top line. Revenue management systems do a lot of things to benefit your business—they produce reports for you, they look out farther into the future than you habitually do, and they provide suitable analytics about pricing, demand, and even incremental revenue in more frequent 'real time'. A GFC, or global pandemic, will always throw a spanner in the works of their calculations, but in 2020 it wasn't just the revenue systems that were out of whack and miscalculating, every human on earth was! Most software options have ways to apply different demand strategies that override the historical data it would normally calculate off of. While an RMS is not essential to a business, they are highly beneficial to saving time on manually updating reports yourself, for the right hotels.

Yes, for the right hotels. This is where an expert revenue consultant can come and provide guidance before a big investment in expensive software is made. I urge hotels not to implement an RMS only for its reporting! I've seen a few regrets from doing that. There are *plenty* of other options to outsource reporting that don't involve such high spend, headache, or set up. RMS systems are not 'set and forget', they are more like robots that still require human intellect and input to understand what's going on (*you* become the art to their science). At a summit I hosted a few years ago now, I likened them to newborn babies—a lot of work but also positively life changing. They are their own individual being but are ultimately their parent's responsibility and require a lot of attention to grow. Perhaps a more appropriate analogy would be the one given to me by a prominent software representative. He said having an RMS is like using cruise-control in a car—maintaining the speed is being done automatically, however the vehicle still needs someone to steer.

Revenue systems are not easy, or set-and-forget, but can also be very rewarding if you are willing to do the work.

Outsource Analytics

Your competitors are a crucial component of your pricing and revenue strategies. The first step is to obtain key analytics about the performance of your handful of opponents in order to compare them against your own, legally of course. There are reliable research companies that compile this information for hotels, Smith Travel Research (STR) being an excellent one of them, whom I've worked with in nearly every hotel. You provide them confidential statistics regarding actual daily revenue performance, and they in turn send you a report comparing your key metrics against an opaque average of your defined group of competitors, as well as figures of the overall market. Participating in STR means your data is never able to be isolated by others, and vice versa, and this mutual trust allows all hotels to confidently contribute and understand their revenue performance better in exchange. Aside from STR, there are many ways to obtain relevant analytics and market research.

If computer systems and data entry aren't your area of expertise, there are plenty of professionals out there who live for this stuff and would be happy to help guide you to make the decision that is best for you and your business. Certainly a software salesmen will show you examples of what their systems can do and how easy it is to navigate, but they are also biased, they are trying to sell. Just like the process of buying a car, you want to receive unbiased reviews of each vehicle, and match it up to your unique needs, before making a big decision on which to choose.

> *This is what a revenue consultant can provide, not only for peace of mind but also to minimise unnecessary mistakes that cost money, time, and team disruption.*

Please don't fret! If I've just given you anxiety with if, what, and how you would get an RMS system, or comparison reports, and who, what or where you find time or resources to manage something like that, you are not alone! I can offer hope and help as you'll soon see in the Outsource chapter, I promise!

4
UNDERSTANDING YOUR BUSINESS

In 'understanding your business' I mean understanding the *money*. And by money, I mean revenue. All that lovely currency that comes through your front door, through hard work, big thoughts, creative ideas, sometimes blood, sweat and even tears—that's revenue. Most of us are in a money-making 'business'. If you charge money for it, then you probably already understand how this works. The labels will differ by industry or region, and the definitions surely vary too. Yet for the most part, this language is relatively universal, especially for industries with the most perishable inventory—hotels, airlines, and rentals of many kinds. This chapter covers the rudiments of Revenue Management.

The Basics

In hotels, revenue is the total amount of dollars you bring in from guest transactions, and it's primarily obtained from what they pay to stay with you, known as the daily room rate, how many rooms they occupy, and for how many nights.

The basic metric of occupancy is typically observed on a percentage basis to allow comparisons to be made with other times of the year, other levels of total inventory (refurbishments or added rooms), and competitor hotels. For newcomers, this might best be illustrated with an example.

If Hotel A, with 10 rooms available to occupy per night, sells 9 rooms to stay on the same night, it will have 90% occupancy for that date.

Likewise, if Hotel B, with 5,000 rooms to sell, occupies 4,000 on a night, they will have 80% occupancy.

If both hotels were the only two in their city, and achieved 100% occupancy on the same night, you would conclude that their 'market' had high demand. Both hotels selling to capacity means hotel A sold 10 rooms, and hotel B sold 5,000. Occupancy as a percentage makes comparing the data of these two hotels more relevant, despite A being a fraction of the size of B.

Occupancy = Total Sold ÷ Total Available to Sell

What you're able to earn per room, on average, based on the prices you sell the rooms at, is called Average Room Rate or Average Daily Rate, abbreviated in acronyms ARR or ADR. This is determined by taking the total room revenue you earned for a night (or month, year, any period) and dividing it by the number of rooms occupied during that same time period.

Average Room/Daily Rate = Total Room Revenue ÷ Total Rooms Sold

This is useful for many reasons, again for the comparison to other hotels or different seasons in the year, but mostly because it averages out all your market segment ADRs and room type prices. The high price of a suite and the low price of a standard room are blended to give you one benchmark number to work towards, for example.

Finally, Revenue Per Available Room, fondly known as RevPAR, is the universal ultimate metric in the hotel world. It levels the playing field for hotels with different strategies and allows us to compare and review their performance against each other with one simple number. So, if one property has a strategy of filling their hotel to 100% occupancy, perhaps by pricing their rooms at a low rate, while another hotel prefers to get high-paying guests even if it means they don't fill all their rooms, this one metric, RevPAR, can tell us who performs better.

From a top-line revenue perspective (remember costs and profit are a different story here) let's expand on the example. If our ten-room hotel is a five-star hotel and can charge $1,000 a night for their rooms, but only fills five rooms a night, that's $5,000 in revenue for its ten available rooms, and a RevPAR of $500. Meanwhile, if the same sized four-star hotel sells at $600 a night over the same night and can sell *all* ten of their rooms, that's $6,000 in revenue, and *$600* in RevPAR. The four-star hotel earned $100 more per available room than the five-star hotel. This could be discussed at length, however the lesson in this example is simply that charging more per room isn't always the way to achieve more revenue per *available* room.

Comparing the RevPAR next to occupancy and ADR allows hoteliers to see the high-level perspective of how well their rooms are selling and where they could improve. Then comparing these results against their STR comp set allows them to further understand if they performed better than their market or left money on the table, so to speak. This then starts the healthy debate of what strategy to work towards—higher rate or higher occupancy. Were it as easy as picking rate or occupancy and then going for it, revenue management would be a much easier practice, and this would be a much shorter book. Unfortunately, while it's not that simple, (nothing good in life ever is) optimizing revenue using fundamental strategies can be satisfying, rewarding, and ignite one's competitive nature.

There are plenty of other metrics and abbreviations that hotels use, such as length of stay, revenue per reservation (total stay, not just per night), total revenue (what they spend per day in your hotel, not just on the accommodation itself), etc. A lot of these are important in their own realms, but for the purpose of sticking to the basics, we'll leave it at occupancy, ADR and RevPAR for now.

We need to understand a few more global terms before we put it all together…

Supply & Demand

For purposes of defining supply and demand in a broader sense, a 'market' refers to all the hotel rooms in the area or region that the property is situated in.
- The 'supply' is the total number of available rooms to sell, in that entire range, on any given night.
- Demand is the number of travellers who want to visit over any given period.

Arguably the hardest factor to forecast, or predict, is demand for a hotel or region, however these days there are many tools and analytics that can assist. Using broader figures from other sources, such as the airline industry, airport statistics, historical indications, even clicks or visitor traffic on your hotel website and the sites your hotel is listed on, can aid in predicting demand.

Producers

Producers of the supply, in this case accommodation units, can fluctuate when new hotels open or older ones close their doors for good. Areas that see strong demand, a surplus of more people interested in staying than available accommodation, are prone to seeing a surge in supply a few years later as developers scurry to capitalize on the increase in visitation. A few years may seem like a long time, but it's the common cycle of property development growth. The witness of strong demand, followed by the decision to build (plus funding, securing land etc.), then planning, designing and developing a new build takes quite some time. New hotels tend to create panic for existing ones nearby, usually for good reason. After all, a new hotel is bright and shiny, and most likely going to offer some great pricing to get people in the door to persuade them to try their product. Their sharp pricing isn't something you can really compete with, because doing so risks permanently eroding ADR by creating the perception of a lesser product in the market.

While it is completely normal to worry about a new competitor, most of the time the best thing to do is be patient and wait for the opening buzz to fade out. In the grand scheme of things, new supply is just a sugar hit.

Excuse me, what? A 'sugar hit'? Yes. When we eat something sugary, our bodies freak out a little, becoming jittery and energized. Then the glucose leaves our system, and our bodies normalize again. This is typically what a new hotel does to a market—creating a temporary dip in the area's occupancy, perhaps rate too, followed by a rebound once constrained demand starts to increase due to higher supply, offering more availability for travellers. Developers seek to build in areas because they observe a *surplus* of demand that they want to capitalize on, not because they want to steal all existing hotel's business. Ultimately, competition is healthy and keeps us striving to be our best.

It takes some time for potential visitors to realise that the city, once too high priced or always fully booked, is now reasonably priced and available again. Thankfully, plenty of tourism campaigns and travel related entities have incentive to get the message out there too. In theory, market supply increases, and their impact on actual demand, might look something like this:

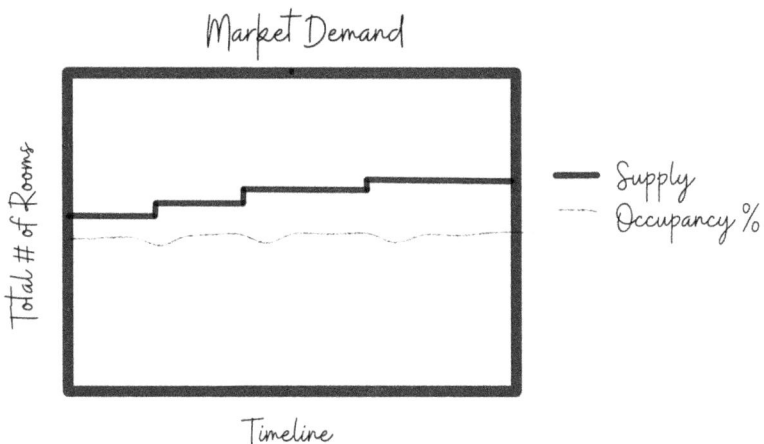

Consumers

Demand is the total amount of willingness and interest there is for consumers to purchase accommodation for a particular date. Generally, the demand for a stay date increases as the arrival date approaches and can be measured as a demand curve. In an unconstrained sense, it's the amount of people who seem to be shopping or interested in booking a room over certain dates, despite what inventory is still available. Constrained demand indicates the actual demand there is if the pricing is agreeable for the buyer. In other words, when a hotel sees a high amount of unconstrained demand, they will implement pricing increases and other restrictions to slow down the demand so it's closer in line with remaining supply while maximizing revenue. Once a market starts to yield their pricing, they 'constrain' the amount of demand coming in over a particular period in line with the remaining supply they have to sell.

Las Vegas over New Year's Eve is a perfect example of the surplus of demand versus the supply of rooms available. Year after year new hotel rooms are built, and repeatedly hotels are virtually full every December 31st.

> *Demand can primarily be controlled through one simple measure—price.*

This is the fundamental law of revenue management—predicting the amount of demand there is for a hotel/market and adjusting the price of the rooms available to sell accordingly. With New Year's Eve in Las Vegas, hotels constrain demand by drastically increasing the price. There's so much demand for that date that different measures can be taken to slow the business down (again with high prices, length of stay restrictions) and *still* fill their establishment to 100% occupancy. In contrast, winter is a notorious season where fewer tourists want to visit, outside of New Year's Eve and any other big events planned of course. In these pockets of low demand and chilly temperatures, hotels promote significantly reduced pricing. Doing this attracts more price-sensitive customers who wouldn't have otherwise been persuaded to visit. It is also when casinos can offer their lower end players much sharper accommodation offers that they don't normally receive at any other time of year.

The measure of 'higher or lower' demand can be observed using Pace. Pace is the speed at which rooms are booking compared to another period, usually prior year. Same Time Last Year (STLY) is a common timestamp measure that provides a guide of whether bookings are ahead or behind the same time last year. Pace of bookings might be behind STLY if you increased pricing this year, for example, in which case you might see ADR pacing ahead of STLY and rooms booked being behind. This could be an intentional shift in strategy from filling rooms at whatever rate possible, the 'heads in beds' method, and shifting to getting the maximum price possible instead.

Pace can be tracked by totalling the number of bookings made each day for a particular stay date to create a Booking Curve. Booking curves can then be overlaid with other periods (the same date last year, midweek or weekend) to better predict where and when the demand will eventuate. Having very few bookings in January for the following New Year's Eve, for example, isn't a reason to panic if your booking curve for last NYE shows that reservations don't start coming in until March, and only really ramp up from October onwards. While they may be easy to understand, booking curves can be difficult to create if you're not saving the right data. The Outsourcing chapter highlights some ideas to make it easier.

Budgets & Forecasts

This all segues nicely into our next basic principles, universal ones—Budgets and Forecasts. Don't roll your eyes just yet, they're not as daunting as you think. If you've never heard of these terms (tell me how that's possible though), a budget is a metric you determine and set for a period, say a month or a year, with expectation or aspiration that you can hit that target. In our personal lives, people often set spending budgets that they try to stay within, keeping them low to increase their savings. In the business world, we set revenue budgets foremost, generally high (sometimes higher than we believe we can achieve) which gives us the benchmark to work towards for the month or year. Most owners like to set them as high as realistically possible in order to maximize revenue and allow for a high valuation of their assets.

If you have experience in the budget process, you'll know that other influences often come into play when it comes to setting one. As a hotelier, you might think you can achieve 3% better revenues above last year, but the financial backer/owner/management group might insist on a more bullish increase. Despite the knee-jerk reaction to believe it's because they're not knowledgeable, it's more likely caused by other elements that exist behind the scenes. Factors such as property loans, appraisals and broader economic or market insights are a few of the motivators that could prompt owners to set loftier budget goals.

A budget is just that—a goal you set with an aim to achieve or exceed. A goal that's put in writing is 42% more likely to be achieved than one that's just spoken about[ix], so how can we fault those who want better for our institution than we believe we can achieve? Sometimes we need a belief that is stronger than our own so that Together Everyone Achieves More (T.E.A.M.).

So, for those of us who have been scorned by slaving over perfecting a budget, to then have it blown out of the water with a much, much higher number, it's time to stop fighting. Accepting a higher benchmark, instead of resisting it, leaves you with energy to pivot, and to figure out how to go about reaching this new bar that's set so beautifully high. Visualise your team hitting that target—imagine the elation, the financial bonus you may receive, the accolades, and the reputation that will carry you to future opportunities, and then put your head down and get to work on making it a reality.

A forecast is what I'll call 'budget lite' in this instance. It's a more fluid version of a budget, updated anywhere from daily to quarterly, and uses more real-time measures of supply and demand to determine what occupancy, ADR and revenue the business will actually achieve. Sometimes it's in line with the budget, sometimes above or below, but typically it's more realistic. Why? Because the budget was set at one point in time, let's say six months before the start of that period, and as we step closer towards the timeframe we start living and breathing the demand in real-time instead of predicting it from so far out.

If a budget is a predictor using last year's data, a forecast is the map to get there by using this year's data to date, the pace, pickup and demand happening for the rest of the year. Good, bad or indifferent, it becomes the more relevant target for the months ahead. In theory, an accurate and well-set budget will run a close parallel with the forecast as the year goes along. Each uses the same set of tools to determine and set the objectives, although unless you're psychic, there's no guarantee they'll stay congruent throughout. Either way, both budgets and forecasts are crucial for mapping out where you expect or hope your business will go. In the words of Benjamin Franklin, "If you fail to plan, you are planning to fail."

The accuracy of budgets and forecasts will improve when you drill down and forecast the subsegments that lie below the high-level metrics of occupancy and rate. Market and channel segments will help you understand the reality of your pricing more than just an aspirational aim of '$XXX in ADR this year'. Market segments have existed since the early days of revenue management, and as the World Wide Web has emerged, so too have channel segments. Today, market and channel labels are often used interchangeably, and are more skewed to channels as the purpose of guest visitation start to blend into several different markets in one stay.

Confused yet? Allow me to back up.

A market segment is most traditionally categorized as business or leisure. A business market segment could include corporate, government, conferences, conventions and anyone deemed as travelling for the purpose of their work. Leisure on the other hand, might stem from a guest on holiday, or on a tour, through a travel agent, with a group of family members, or as part of a wedding. Travel for pleasure = leisure.

Channels are the way in which these bookings were made. Did they funnel through the hotel's website, or a third-party site known as an online travel agent (OTA)? Were they made directly through the hotel's reservations team, or via a traditional travel agent and the global distribution system (GDS)? There are many market segments and booking methods that can identify as channels, which is why it's up to each hotel or group to determine which are most important and relevant for them. Any group of individuals that have similar buying behaviours and can be influenced using your sales and marketing efforts should definitely be segmented and forecasted in your business.

To complicate things, travel today has started to become part business/part leisure (bleisure), and booking methods aren't as traditional as they used to be. A corporate traveller may book through an OTA, where traditionally only leisure business would book their stays. Likewise, a holiday guest might reserve via a corporate travel agent because it provides ease of book-ability, they are accustomed to this method for their work travel. This makes forecasting purely by market or channel difficult, as the identifiers of guests currently categorised into these segments are likely to evolve and change as travel habits and booking methods evolve and change too.

What's important, for purposes of forecasting and pricing particularly, is to have a like-for-like measure of each segment to compare with over time. It's easier to decide if your OTA bookings will increase or decrease this year if you've always labelled reservations coming through this channel as 'OTA' and can see how they are pacing against STLY, for example. If all your conference bookings have been labelled as 'Meetings & Events', and perhaps are even sub-segmented to more distinct categories (in-hotel conference, external conference, association event, incentive trips, etc.) it will help you to map which one you need to target more or less of to improve on prior year's results. It doesn't matter what you categorize your segments as, so long as you keep them consistent and relevant. In order to influence performance through marketing tactics, you must maintain accurate year-on-year comparisons.

Base Business

Base business is critical to the optimization of your business, particularly in hospitality and retail. It's the stuff you sell at a discounted price point, knowing it brings in some volume and gives you leverage to put stronger prices out in the public market as you've got some 'base on the books'. It's the foundation that strengthens your backbone to push rates up, because you know that if all else fails, and no one wants to pay the higher pricing, you at least already have some base business to rely on for revenue.

Base business is a balance, however. There's a fine line between taking too much at too low a price, not taking enough and missing out on maximizing income. The sweet spot in-between is always where we find the most profitable days for hotels.

"Okay, so how do we get there?" you ask. Through analytics, and trial and error.

Every business is different, and every 'base' is comprised of unique market or channel segments that are best suited for each hotel. A resort may consider wholesale groups (guests travelling with a tour guide, paying discounted room rates because they've booked the entire trip as a package) as their base business. Generally, wholesale agents are offered reduced pricing, flat rate or percentage discounted, because they promise (and hopefully prove) to bring in a high volume of rooms to your hotel all year long. Similarly, in a more business-oriented hotel, base business might be corporate contracted travel that commits to bring in a high volume of rooms throughout the year too. Likewise, lower rates are offered to conference business, knowing they will certainly make up for the discount in accommodation revenue with what they spend on meeting room hire, catering, and food and beverage.

> *Knowing which type of business, and how much, can take some time to get right.*
> *The easiest way to figure out the best market mix or base business for your hotel is to start by looking at your best performing dates, months and seasons.*
> *Identify what market or channel segments contributed to those successes and apply a similar strategy to your budgets and forecasts moving forward.*

Was wholesale 30% of your occupancy on those dates? Good, start there. Or perhaps conferencing and events made up 40% of your business over that period? Perfect, rally your sales team to target the same type of groups again. Then step through those periods and analyse the results—did it perform well against the prior year? Better? Great, keep the formula of whatever market segment percentages you had going. If it was worse, drill down into all the details. Was the conference secured at too low a rate? Did they not materialize the way you thought they would? Next year you'll know to commit more business beforehand, knowing that some of it will wash, or not show up in full.

The beauty about all of this is that if you look carefully at the data, you have a greater opportunity to maximize your room rate potential above and beyond the prior year with better revenue management. Using the key levers of pricing, inventory, marketing and distribution, you'll steer your ship in the [profitable] direction you want it to go.

I hope by now you understand the importance of understanding your business. Not just what it's about, or how you got there, but also what it's comprised of, what its goals are, it's mission statement that everyone uses to align their efforts towards. It's so easy to find it hard to stay the course when there are so many insignificant distractions vying for your time at every moment. Understanding the depth and breadth of the purpose of the business you built or are working in, and the desire of it contributing to society in a way that mirrors your values, that is the mission. This should always be the goal.

5
PRICING & PRODUCT

The simplicity of defining what a product is (that which you're selling), and a price (what you charge for what you're selling), is very deceiving once you've scratched the surface of everything that can go into them. In hotels, we generally price rooms independently and then assume (hope) enough of these guests will spend money at our outlets instead of venturing offsite. Luckily for resorts, it's a more captive audience in that guests generally stay, and spend, on-site much more.

You'd likely suggest a resort might price their rooms more competitively than a hotel, knowing they'll retain the guest (and their money) more than a city hotel, where the options to eat and drink are endless. However, there are a myriad of other factors that determine how you set your rate. What's your product's reputation like? How does it compare to others nearby—is it better or worse? Are customers loyal to your product? Do you have a loyalty program to entice them to pick you versus the 'not you' next door?

I once had an analyst work for me who came from the cruise line industry. There are so many parallels to hotels—both have rooms, theirs just happen to float around the world. But the pricing philosophy of cruise ships is different to hotels because they know if they offer a discount on the accommodation portion, it gives their customer more spending money while they're on the ship. They also know that getting people on a cruise practically guarantees they'll spend money with them on board. Why? Because they're trapped, or should I say sailing, often at sea for days at a time without a glimmer of land in sight. What else is there to do?

The revenue brain of mine often wishes we could lock our hotel doors after guests arrive and just let them spend away, although on land that's usually known as a hostage situation, so... never mind. Resorts behave more like a cruise line, while hotels are more like an airline. Regardless of the product, they all have lots of competition and need to differentiate themselves to win the business of their customers.

Know Your Worth

The key to pricing appropriately in any industry is to know your worth, how you differ from everyone else, and then stand behind those differences and own them unconditionally. We should do this in life as well. Figure out your unique qualities, stand up tall, and don't settle for anything less than you deserve. I suppose this could suggest you hire an egomaniac who is as passionate about your product as he/she is his/her own. You could, but you don't have to. Instead, you just need to know your BATNA.

> *BATNA. An acronym for the 'Best Alternative to a Negotiated Agreement'.*

Huh? In other words, determine the most advantageous alternative your customer would take if they didn't choose your product. Understanding your property, and your competitors, from every angle will help you prepare for the conversations and negotiations a client might present and combat them with ease. Maybe your hotel doesn't have as much meeting space as others, so you partner with a local convention hall to have an option for increased space. Perhaps you don't have a gym on-site, so you work out a deal with the big fancy one nearby and highlight it as a feature, 'complimentary access to state-of-the-art fitness equipment and classes at XYZ FIT next door'.

You also want to understand what great qualities your product has that no one else does. Is it a rooftop pool where wedding receptions can be held, or an award-winning restaurant? Knowing what you and your competitors have in common, and in contrast, helps you defend your product as the best option without hesitation. It also helps eliminate your team from negotiating *against themselves*, especially when it comes to pricing. Knowing your worth means when a customer tries the "well, your competitor is going to give this to me for $20 cheaper," card, they can rattle off an assured response with all the reasons why you're worth $20 more, instead of them panicking about losing the business and adjusting their original quote down by $20 to match.

That's what I mean by negotiating against yourself. If you've priced appropriately the first time, you should never have to settle for something less without bartering for something else that you want instead. An example would be to insist that the only way you could offer a lower rate for product A is if they agree to purchase product B as well. In hotels this might be giving a wedding party $20 off their room rate if they agree to host their reception at the hotel, perhaps with a minimum spend requirement. Or to hold strong on pricing and offering something of value to the client (but of little or no cost to you,) such as maintaining the $20 higher rate but offering late checkout of 4pm for free, perhaps.

I was invited to attend a negotiation course by a previous employer, and I'd highly recommend it for absolutely anyone and everyone. I was reluctant to go. I'm not in sales, I'd already negotiated my contracted commissions as low as they could be, what was the point? However, when you stop and think about just how many things we all negotiate in our personal lives, from furniture to utilities, tradesmen to treatments, you start to develop a more confident bartering muscle. Knowing your BATNA and doing a SWOT analysis (Strengths, Weaknesses, Opportunities, Threats) will help you price more appropriately, appreciate the financial contributions you make to those businesses, and ultimately bring in the most revenue possible.

Market Research

This usually refers to the broader scope of a hotel's 'market' rather than just the nearby hotels, however it can also be both. A 'market' is a way to categorise other hotels with similar attributes into a group. It could be the city the hotel is in, or a region/country where the same type of hotel has similar qualities to yours, wellness retreats, or conference hotels, for example. A market could also be a handful of nearby hotels that have a similar number of rooms, type of hotel (business, convention, resort), quality or star rating. When it is a handful of hotels, considered to be a direct competitor to your business, it is referred to as a **'competitive set' or 'comp set'**. A hotel that has potential to take business away from your hotel and into theirs, and contains several commonalities to yours, would typically be part of your competitive set. Put simply, the set of hotels that you directly compete with.

As introduced in the previous chapter, in my experience, the easiest and best way to do this is by working with Smith Travel Research (STR) or a similar provider if they aren't prominent in your region. STR works with nearly all hotels in Australia, which means each property sends their revenue and occupancy data, and they in turn produce reports that show your results compared with the blended average of your chosen comp set hotels. Genius! They maintain the privacy of each hotel and have numerous practices in place to prevent anyone from finding a way to isolate other hotels' data as well. They are easy to work, with and have powerful reporting and insights that can help you make better pricing decisions. Hotels can create multiple comp set groups to gain a better understanding of how they perform against different types of competitors.

STR also provides a wealth of information and education to the hotel industry and have always been a reliable resource of market research of the numerical kind. The tools and dashboards that they have created are extremely insightful and can help properties determine their market positioning more easily. As a revenue manager, the favoured metric are the indexes. Put simply, STR divides your hotel's result (in occupancy, ADR, and RevPAR) with the averaged result of your comp set. If this index is above 1.0 it means you achieved more than your fair share compared to your competitors. If your index is below 1.0 then your competitors outperformed you. Looking at the indexes for each night for occupancy and ADR provides a solid indication of what night you should have pushed rate more, and what nights your pricing may have been too high when compared to how much more occupancy the index is implying your comp set achieved. STR is a data powerhouse and can provide so much support to your revenue decisions, far beyond what I've described. I highly recommend subscribing to their reporting, the value far outweighs the cost. It is so powerful to understand how your competitors are performing, especially these days when attracting guests to travel is much harder work.

Pricing

How you price your product is the ultimate key to your business's success. Set it too high, and you alienate your potential buyers from giving you their money. Too low and you leave money on the table, or worse, you devalue your product by people thinking it's cheap. How to figure out the right price point is no easy feat, but the most important thing is to try, and to keep trying until you find what works for you.

There are an endless amount of factors that can be used to determine price. Where are you located? What are your unique selling points that attract people to your hotel instead of others? What are your competitor rates, and are they superior or lesser than your product? How are your guest reviews compared to theirs? What are the consistent themes in the reviews you receive—for example, too expensive, or good value?

That's just the tip of the iceberg though because supply and demand play a vital role too. How busy is your establishment on any given night of the week, and how busy are your competitors or your market?

There are many ways to get statistics about a city, or a set of competitor hotels, via STR and other data intelligence companies. Even visitation and airline passenger numbers can provide answers to this question. Comparing your situation to the same time last year, what occupancy you finished at for that period, is also a crucial way to understand how you could perform this year. And then there's cost—what's the minimum amount you need to sell a room at in order to cover your costs? Hopefully your selling price is well above that number, but it's always crucial to keep in mind regardless, especially when considering promotions that would discount your selling rate. Things like taxes, commission and costs of marketing also need to be factored there's a lot involved.

The best way to go about setting your prices is with a hotel management strategy meeting. Gather your numbers people (finance, revenue, front office even) and your sales people (sales, marketing, reservations, etc.) and together discuss, research, review and decide on a pricing structure that works for your hotel. This doesn't need to be rigid or set in stone, but it should at least include the lowest and highest rates you're willing to sell at. The rest can be tested through different trials down the track.

You may also want to discuss 'vanity' prices, such as, will you end all your prices in a 0 or a 9? Will you include decimals, or cents, or round up or down to the nearest dollar? There are studies that can give insights of the attraction of whether $99 or $100 sells better or worse, but ultimately the decision is yours to make. People will still stay with you for $100 if your price is competitively set against the myriad of factors already mentioned. Do what you feel is best for your hotel and peace of mind and remember it can always be modified later.

Static & Dynamic

The next element of pricing to consider is whether you'll have static or just dynamic rates. Static rates are typically seasonal, perhaps split by midweek and weekend, they don't go up or down when there's more or less demand once they're set, whereas dynamic prices do. Dynamic rates are more reactive to immediate market conditions, so stronger than anticipated demand means you can flex your prices up as your availability diminishes. Static rates on the other hand, typically only go 'on or off'. If you have too much demand, you stop selling them. When the market is unusually slow, you can reduce them, but then it becomes difficult to get them back up or above what they were originally set at.

Why is this, and who says so? Great question, and one I could debate about all day long, but I won't. Instead, and in short, rates that are static are beneficial for businesses and travel agents who send guests to your hotel. Corporations can contract static negotiated rates in exchange for sending a high volume of room nights to your hotel. They typically like, or need, a fixed rate because they have travel budgets they must adhere to. Leisure travel companies, such as agents, tours or wholesalers, request static rates so they have control over the accuracy and transparency in their travel brochures. No one likes to see a hotel advertised for one price, only to find the amount is higher when they go to book the room. This makes sense, but this is also what I would call 'legacy' pricing, and in my opinion, should be evolving to a more fluid method much faster by now than it has been.

Brochures are a logical reason to set static rates, true, but when was the last time the majority of the travelling population looked at a paper brochure to travel? Yes, there's still a demand and a market for such visitors, but for the most part, researching where to stay is done online, which is as dynamic a platform as you can get. If a brochure simply put the word 'From' in front of the price, it would give the hotel flexibility to flex/adjust prices as needed, and it would give the consumer the understanding that this price *could* be the rate, or that it may be higher. Seems very logical, and yet for the most part this isn't an accepted practice by leisure on-sellers. Hotels find themselves either opting in for selling static rates, as well as dynamic, or avoiding contracting with the tour and travel segments entirely.

We'll cover more about why a hotel would choose to opt out of working with them in the next chapter, for now let's look at the downside of having both pricing models in play.

Static

A static rate is set lower (typically very low) than you would want to sell for publicly (retail sales) in exchange for a high volume of guaranteed room nights booking your hotel. Traditionally, leisure travellers were assumed to be the ones staying on wholesale rates, at prices up to or around 30% less than your typical public rate.

In the business world, room discounts are commonly known as Corporate Negotiated Rates, and can vary in price depending on the volume of business their company anticipates and the days of the week their travellers will be staying.

Corporate rates are also determined by whether or not a 'last room availability' (LRA) is part of the agreement. An LRA means if the hotel has only one room left to sell, and they've priced it extremely high publicly, knowing it will book quickly, the hotel is still obligated to take the corporate guests at their lower rate because of the LRA agreement in their contract. This type of guarantee typically means that the rate negotiated is slightly higher than a non-LRA agreement, however considering they are assured a fixed price no matter what the market demand is dictating, it's an exchange corporations with frequent travel are willing to make.

A non-LRA agreement has benefits for both parties as well. The hotel can flex the availability of the contracted rate by closing it when they're starting to fill up, then sell at much higher prices in response to much higher demand. The corporate customer who usually gets a lower price than most on most days, is willing to pay a retail or full rate every so often or choose other travel dates when theirs isn't available. A non-LRA agreement also encourages them to book their reservations as far in advance as possible to ensure their price is available. The farther out we can get guests to book, the better prepared we can be to maximize revenue leading up to the day of arrival.

The problem with having static and dynamic rates, however, is that sometimes these price points overlap and cause problems with the parties you're doing business with. See below:

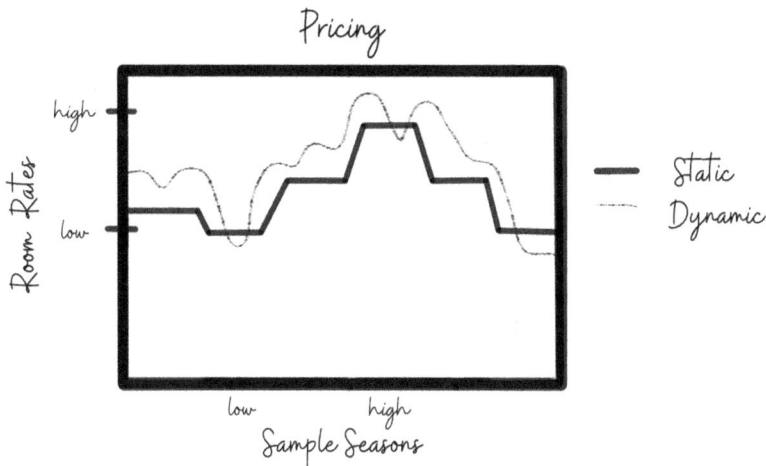

In this example, the static prices hardly move. They're seasonal, set for the year well in advance, and almost always before hotels have a clear understanding of the market demand ahead. The static rates might be for a group, conference, leisure travel agent (wholesale), corporate or government business, even an online booking agent or group buying website. Most of these entities, or those acting as an agent (i.e., with exception of conferences and corporations) will mark up the negotiated static price you've given them. That's how they make their respective revenue. Hotels give them a static rate of $100 and both parties agree the agent should mark up the price by a certain percent, let's say 25%, so the selling rate the end consumer will see is $125. The hotel gets $100, and the agent keeps $25.

Dynamic

Meanwhile, the dynamic pricing determined is fluctuating daily as needed. Each property looks at the number of people looking at or booking their hotel for every date, how competitor hotels are changing their pricing (taking rates up or down) and adjusts rates accordingly. In a busy period, all is fine for the contractors of negotiated static rates as they're getting good value compared to the high public prices. Consumers are buying through them because their prices are lower. All is well ... for them. However, in slower than anticipated periods where rooms aren't selling so fast, the dynamic structure gives hotels the flexibility to take their prices down to try and stimulate demand. This often results in selling at lower prices than their static ones, which upsets those contracted recipients who have fixed, and now higher, rates than what is available publicly.

This can lead to a myriad of issues, including rate parity concerns. The problem with having static and dynamic rates selling at the same time means there's a lot more to keep track of, and more challenges with keeping a consistent message that *endorses your brand integrity.*

While there's value in both static and dynamic structures, I'm inclined to support dynamic pricing's flexibility more strongly than the steadfastness of static. Dynamic means you're able to be nimbler when unforeseen changes arise. You can go up, down and everywhere in-between based on each day's respective demand level. There can still be promotions or discounts in play, they just sit as a percentage off your dynamic rate instead of being set at a fixed lower price. At the end of the day, the more hotels can automate, simplify and control, the better control they have of their distribution, reputation and ultimately, their revenue.

Product

Commerce has been around for centuries, so exploring how pricing has been done previously, and in similar industries to your own, could be greatly beneficial to your business. Imitation is a form of flattery, and in many respects there truly is no need to reinvent (or complicate) the wheel. Hotels derived their revenue management principals from the airline industry, but often I feel we've drifted too far away from our aviation roots. Time and again, when you book a room, you'll see the pricing page of the hotel's website full of, and I mean swimming with, prices, packages, promotions and room types. This makes it difficult and overwhelming for a consumer to decide which one to choose. We tend to assume guests understand our lingo more than I believe they actually do, and that they instinctively know the difference between our room types, inclusions and restrictions of each price we offer. Less is always more and understanding what truly compels buyers to book is paramount. We'll cover off how to streamline your offers next, but first let's talk about the products themselves.

The Product

If packages, promotions and offers are the wrapping paper, your product is the gift. Chances are you already have a few different variations of your offering. In hotels, it's usually size and amenities based, categorised into room types. Many hotels have 'entry level' or 'run of house' room types, the baseline product it offers. Next up could be a superior room type, better than a standard room in various ways, perhaps slightly bigger, or has a better view, on a higher floor. Then, it's typically a 'deluxe' room, then suites. In airlines it's largely economy, business, then first class. In a mobile phone world, it's the size and then storage capacity of your device. Added amenities could be a myriad of things, but most importantly they are elements that *consumers are willing to pay more for.*

Most businesses have more than one variety of their product, which expands the buying audience and generates more sales. The key to differentiating your product types and promotions, as you'll see later, is to keep them clean and simple. I once worked with a hotel that had more than thirty different room types and only a few hundred rooms! They had a different type for each size room, for which way the room was facing, if it had a bath or shower or both—the list went on and on.

At a minimum, hotel guests will want to know what size bed they're getting and if there's a bath or shower before they commit to buy. And that's it! The rest is just icing, icing they may be willing to pay for, sure, but not mission critical to their visit. A person booking a business class flight will want to know they have a bigger seat and upgraded amenities and service, but whether beef or chicken will be served on the flight isn't going to heavily influence their decision to book, if at all.

Whenever a hotel gets carried away with creating a buffet of room types, I circle back to airline websites. Typically, they'll have three to four different classes (premium economy, business, etc.) and three to four different options for each—a saver deal (making changes are difficult), a flexi offer (making changes are easier) and perhaps a rewards deal (pay with your loyalty points) and that's it! Sure, some low-cost carriers might bundle luggage and or meals (we'll call these packages), but typically airlines will simply say, "pick your seat type, and pick what's important to you—lower price or higher flexibility." The end. It makes things easier, as you don't have to sift through pages of deals, it's just a take it or leave it approach. The consumer can choose the brand, and the product that best suits their needs, or to go to another airline. And that's okay, because there might be just as many visitors on the competitor sites deciding if they'll commit or continue to shop around.

It's not just price—reputation, reviews, loyalty and service also influence the decision-making process of our consumers, and those are more difficult, if not impossible, to put a true value on.

Packages & Promotions

Packages and promotions are often combined into a unanimous category, however they serve different purposes. Packages can be used in a promotion to create an attractive offer and bring in bookings. A promotion can be a booking window, or time frame, that gives the customer a *call to action* to book. It can also be a price point offer, usually discounted, maybe a few value-adds thrown in, with a limited booking period, to create urgency. Think of it like this – if packages are the movie stars, promotions are their talent agents.

Packages

Generally speaking, packages are designed to bundle elements to create a compelling reason to buy, primarily from a marketing and advertising perspective. You want more people to know you have a spa, or to try your restaurant, so you put those elements in your bundle. Packages can then be promoted, or marketed, through numerous travel platforms as a unique offering, with a new catchy (and concise) name like 'Spa Indulgence' package. Public relations teams then use packages to create a story about the hotel, showcasing your products in various mediums while enticing each audience with an attractive reason to try your hotel.

Mainstream media, such as travel magazines, newspapers and travel centric tv shows are where you'd expect to see these offers display. The packages aren't necessarily cheap or heavily discounted, however they usually do give buyers a better deal on each element. Bundling it together into one amount creates a higher price point overall, therefore disguising the discount applied to each individual item. This is ideal, as it maintains brand integrity by ensuring each component's rate reduction is opaque.

As an example, if breakfast at your hotel is normally $25, and the room rate is $180 for the night, you might bundle them at $200 to create a 'Bed & Breakfast' package. The guest receives a lower price for breakfast (in this case $5), the hotel has locked in extra revenue for the restaurant before arrival and has an indication of number of covers in advance. Package elements like monetary 'credits', designed for guests to use in the hotel during their stay, are also attractive, because they don't limit the customer into one option such as breakfast, but they do lock them into staying (and spending) in the hotel. One guest may choose to use their $50 credit at the bar or restaurant, while another might put it towards a spa treatment. Chances are they'll end up spending more money at your property than the credit amount they received, I'm guilty of that myself.

My advice with all products and pricing is to keep them simple, for the benefit of the consumer *and* the hotel team. Making an offer so loaded with things that it's confusing and hard to understand if there's value is a nightmare. Don't put so many fences, or restrictions, around a promotion that it's difficult to persuade someone to book it. Consumers want to easily understand there's a good offer on the table, and that it's compelling enough to either pay a higher price for (package) or commit to buying it straight away (promotion) to lock in the best price.

What if you already have packages? Sure, you say, they're a little complex, but they get booked from time to time? Doesn't that count? Great question. This is when you need to analyse *when* customers are booking and *why*, then break down the revenue potential of each component. It's the only way you'll understand if it's truly maximizing revenue for your hotel.

For example, say you have a nice, complex 'Pamper & Indulge' offer at your property. It includes a ninety-minute spa treatment, breakfast for two daily, a $50 resort credit, a bottle of champagne on arrival, and is priced at $400 a night. "$400 revenue, woo hoo!" you think! And you're right—but only if it's booked for nights that you're *not* going to fill to 100% occupancy.

Now you're thinking I'm absurd to discredit $400 in revenue like that, but let's break down the package components using simple numbers as an example:

Spa Treatment 90 minutes	$150
Breakfast for two ($25 per person)	$50
Resort Credit	$50
Bottle of champagne	$50
Which leaves nightly Room Revenue at:	**$100**
Total Package Price	$400

Is this package beneficial or harmful to your hotel? Don't answer that—it's a trick question!

When the hotel runs at historically low occupancies, as in you wouldn't even be able to give the rooms away for free because there's minimal interest in your city at that time of year, then absolutely, let's fill it up with $400 packages. It means the hotel outlets get some money, and the accommodation side gets $100 in revenue. Even if the cost per occupied room is $70, that's still a 30% margin, which is great. If, however, we're looking at the busiest times of year, and you notice that's when this package always seems to stay (on Saturday nights and New Year's Eve for example), are you happy with $100 for a room you could have otherwise sold for at least double? I would think not.

The key to building a package is deciding which components are going to be team players and take one for the team, and which are going to reap the benefits of being bundled. Say your spa isn't attracting many guests in-house and is losing profits because keeping your massage therapists employed is costly when there's no revenue coming in. Then the big picture tactic might be to take a room at $100 for the sake of giving the spa $150 in revenue. Because a package is … packaged, a guest will never know they're getting a $100 room rate. They might think they've paid the more common price of $200 for the room and are getting the ninety-minute spa treatment for $50! They'll never know.

And that's the beauty of packages. They allow you to discount elements of your hotel while maintaining pricing integrity (this hotel would probably _never_ price their hotel rooms at $100 publicly). However, with this bundling benefit comes greater responsibility for controlling availability. That means making packages unavailable over busy periods when their help isn't needed, and constantly monitoring when they do book to ensure it's still for a beneficial stay date—yielding or closing them when you don't need the help any longer, and keeping them open when you do.

But there's a problem with this—if you've closed the offer for half of the year, it'll frustrate the consumer when they can rarely find it available, not to mention the plausible pitfall of false advertising. If, however, you showcase this package as 'From $400' instead of a static price, then you can flex the room rate so it's almost always available, just at different price points throughout the year. Always ensure the customer can see a benefit of booking it, as in being able to tell it's good value. If every element in your package is at full retail price, including the room rate, what's enticing them to book it as a bundle instead of individually? Sometimes just a 5% discount is enough to convince them to buy. Also be sure that there are ample dates at the 'starting from' price point available to prevent it from being misleading. Play around with what you create, just be sure to monitor and adjust as needed.

Promotions

Promotions are usually more transparent than packages and typically offer a deeper discount, perhaps with a few low, or 'soft' cost value-adds like complimentary late checkout or room upgrade, in exchange for some kind of commitment from the consumer, like requiring full pre-payment or making the offer non-refundable. Creating an urgent call to action, like 'book before this date' or 'while supplies last/subject to availability' means they're also able to be marketed and advertised but are more time sensitive and persuade the guest to book quickly. Offers should be easy to understand—both when they are available to book *and stay*—to avoid confusion for the guest, and the hotel team too.

Limited Time Only (LTO) offers are the best way to give sharp discounts without overexposing a risk of giving away revenue (i.e., taking a lower rate when you could have yielded and taken a higher one). If you still need help when the promotion ends, you can do it again, perhaps at a slightly higher rate, or extend the 'reserve by' date. If you booked plenty on the original offer and don't need any more help at discounted rates, you close it out as planned and coast the rest of the way, yielding your normal public rates.

Packages and promotions are a great and fun way to get creative with unique and attractive offers your guests will enjoy. Just avoid getting too carried away, and don't reinvent the wheel. If your existing offers are generating a nice amount of interest *and* revenue, leave them alone. The bed and breakfast offer will likely remain a staple in the hotel industry for eternity, so why change it? Get inventive, just don't get so complex that no one, including the hotel team, understands what's on offer. And do your best not to make it too complicated to execute at the hotel level either.

In my early days as a revenue manager, I once created an offer that included a rental car with the room. Nothing wrong with that, it did quite well, however it required constant monitoring of bookings, then contacting the guest for details on their flights, and lastly liaising with the rental car agency to book the vehicle. Unique? Yes. Attractive? Yes. A lot of work required in the background and risk of guest dissatisfaction if it wasn't executed properly? Yes, exactly. You get the point.

Use packages and promotions to your financial benefit, be sure to think big picture, and don't overdo it. Having too many bells and whistles out there at any given time will give the consumer analysis paralysis, not knowing which one is best or what to book. The decision should be easy for them. They shouldn't need to work hard to pencil out and process the benefits. As a rule of thumb, I suggest no more than three offers, packages or promotions be available to book at any given time. I often refer to a wine menu example when thinking about what to make available. As in, when you're at a restaurant and looking at the wine menu, reviewing which one to choose, what do people go for? Most patrons won't choose the cheapest bottle, it's probably not any good, and they won't choose the most expensive because they decide it's overpriced or over their budget. Instead, *they choose the middle option,* not too high, not too low, but just right. Keep this in mind when you create offers. Of course, you'll have guests choose the cheapest, and the most expensive (keep those), but the majority will fall in-between. Decide what you need that number to be, then create the ideal deal with one above and below it.

Airbnb

So, you have your product—in this case it's rooms. So do others nearby, all known as your *competition* (those you compete against to get business, whatever business it may be, to get customers to buy your product instead of theirs). Competitors come in all shapes and sizes, and ever more so as the sharing economy continues to grow. People considering a hotel stay previously would have looked at similar nearby hotels, then possibly up or down in rating or scale (motel versus hotel, etc.) and that would be it. Today though, there's Airbnb as the subtle opponent, offering unique accommodation options and often more competitively priced, especially when hotels are filling up fast because of high demand over busy periods. Holiday rental owners continue to create points of difference with their type of offering, like staying in boats or tree houses. It's hard to compete with a tree house, no matter who you are.

What are you supposed to do? Price the same (or lower) than the neighbouring hotel to win the business? You'd think so, but no. Panic about Airbnb and drop prices and strip back amenities? You could, but you should also understand that it's ultimately a different demographic who's attracted to that type of accommodation, no matter how similar they may seem. Sure, a guest looking for a place to stay could be looking at hotels *and* houses, but ultimately those looking for traditional services and securities, such as daily housekeeping, staff members on-site 24/7, room service and cleaning standards are always going to favour hotels over other people's homes. Likewise, those who want to travel in packs, cook for themselves and feel as if they're in a 'home away from home', albeit someone else's, will gravitate towards Airbnb every time, hotels don't stand a chance.

Both accommodation styles are similar, but vastly different. Owning and standing confidently in these differences is paramount. Sure, guests might switch between the two types depending on availability, cost and location, but that's about it. When I travel for business, I want a nice, clean, quiet room where I can get work done without distractions, can pop downstairs for a meal or exercise, and then use my room as a hub between meetings and appointments.

When on holiday for a best friend's wedding, sharing a house seems like a decent idea, and so we did. We could all gather, cook and catch up. But I'll just say this—these 'house hotels' are not regulated to anywhere near the same level as hotels. My experience in them has never been as good as places that are operated by hospitality experts. Large fuzzy bathmats that you know aren't easily washable under my feet, ick. Bed linens that look and feel like they may not have been washed, I can't be sure. Even a newly refurbished apartment I stayed at in Cannes presented issues, with a brand-new dishwasher that didn't work, ants trailing everywhere, and a master bedroom without proper curtains to block out the light. Sure, that can be reconciled, and a bottle of champagne was a nice gesture for my inconvenience of draping blankets over the thin window coverings. However, that's always a lot more hassle compared to picking up the phone to tell the hotel staff you're not satisfied.

You might think I'm not a fan of sharing accommodation companies, but that's not true! They have a purpose and a place for a demographic that aren't necessarily happy at a hotel, and that's wonderful. They can nestle you into the heart of niche locations that you wouldn't otherwise get to immerse yourself in so you can live like a local. They offer alternatives to desperate travellers when all the hotels are fully booked, and they offer a revenue stream to the residents who normally live in them. But I'll always be a hotelier at heart, and what I will say is that I don't believe Airbnb is as much of a threat or competitor to the majority of hotels and resorts as we speculate it is. Not like we thought they would be, at least. It was an initial sugar hit that has gradually stabilized. There will be exceptions to this rule, there always are. I believe Airbnb has a place in this industry, and so do hotels, the latter always will.

The Price is Right

There are a million different ways to slice, dice and price your products, promotions and hotel offerings. There are also a million different ways to price in general—static (seasonal), dynamic (fluctuates daily), or both. And there's the vanity debate—does ending your price in a 9 or a 0 see more products sell? Is $99 more compelling than $100, or does it not matter? Are consumers more drawn towards a discounted percentage or a dollar amount? Save 20% or save $20? The answer isn't black and white, and never one size fits all either. Just as some people are data driven and others are visual, you'll have different responses to your offering because everyone is different, and that's okay. Test the waters, try one, do both, review, revisit, adjust. Lean on your team around you for input and ideas.

Out in the world, a million different products are priced a million different ways, and they all sell in one way or another. Go with your intuition, and if it proves to be wrong, too successful, or not successful enough, change it. It's that simple. The more you test ideas, the more you'll understand what's right for your business.

6
DISTRIBUTION

Distribution: "the process of making a product or service available for the consumer or business user who needs it. This can be done directly by the producer or service provider or using indirect channels with distributors or intermediaries."[x]

Distribution started out as simple and straightforward years ago, but with the emergence of the Internet, new players, and new ways of booking a room, it's now much more complex. Managing these distributors of hotel products (as in who would sell it, and what sites would you entrust to sell it, etc.) became a prominent component of a revenue manager's responsibilities well over a decade ago. So much so that many revenue related job titles expanded to 'Revenue & Distribution', including my own. Revenue is revenue, and pricing is one thing, but distribution suddenly came with needs all its own, hence the reason a separate distinguishable identifier was necessary.

The simple snapshot of distribution is deciding what channels to sell your rooms through. The integrity of each is a paramount consideration, along with the scope or reach they have to an audience you likely wouldn't get to otherwise, and the cost of doing business through each channel.

Sources

In hospitality, the most traditional channels are described as:
- Hotel Direct: *Guests call, email, or walk into your hotel to book a room.*
- Brand.com: *Guest goes onto your hotel's website and books a room via your booking engine on your proprietary URL (hosted and managed by your business).*
- Online Travel Agent (OTA): *Guests go onto travel websites, find your hotel amongst many others displayed, and book a room via that booking engine. You'd know the most prominent players as Booking.com and Expedia (written here solely alphabetically), but there are thousands of others as well.*
- Global Distribution System (GDS): *Arguably a version of the Internet before the World Wide Web emerged, this is a system that consists of key distributors—Sabre, Amadeus and Travelport.*

GDS allows travel agents to book multiple components of travel, such as hotel and airfare, for guests travelling for leisure or business. In the corporate world, companies typically engage a large agent called a Travel Management Company (TMC) or Consortia to help book their travel needs. Think of them as an element layered on top of the GDS. TMCs command buying power because of the volumes they produce for hotels, primarily with business related travellers, and usually operate via a GDS. Hotels typically pay the TMCs a fee to be included in their system, sometimes offer room discounts, and pay a processing fee to the GDS for each reservation in addition. Stays made via the GDS channel often accrue the highest costs per booking, however also tend to generate the highest revenues, room rates, and ancillary spend on-site, which is why they are still considered a very valuable source of business.

While these are the four main channels, and the labels may vary slightly, the way technology and access to each platform has evolved, with many distributors now able to access inventory from multiple platforms, means there's a substantial amount of overlap between each channel and what prices they can access to distribute. This can make it difficult to control what price point is publicly available at your hotel.

Channels

If you're overwhelmed by the notion of managing each of these channels individually, I don't blame you! Thankfully, there are solutions to assist. Please don't skip over this chapter, *everyone* needs to have some idea of how it all works, because each component is a revenue source for your hotel, and revenue is ultimate. The best leaders I've worked for have always had a solid understanding of how distribution works. If you're an accommodation owner, consider this the one chapter that you just need to get through no matter what. Know the acronyms, understand the key players, then move on and feel better knowing you can 'talk the talk' with whomever you delegate this to. Stay with me, because if I can understand it anyone can, I promise. I will soon explain how to manage this with minimal stress (spoiler alert—don't do it yourself, outsource it!)

We've learned how the distribution of hotel products (rooms) occurs through various channels, within which are a multitude of different market segments that drive the bookings. Typically, this is where I would show you how each market slots into a corresponding channel, but I can't any longer as they are ever-changing and evolving to adapt to new booking methods. Comparable to distribution sources via channels, with the emergence of improved technology, many of these market segments now overlap into more than one booking source. While this makes for good revenue maximizing on your distributors' side, it creates a very confusing scenario for the hotel.

For example, a traditional travel agent (with a storefront that you walk into and browse brochures) may have contracted static wholesale rates with a hotel, to bundle or mark up with flights etc., and on-sell to consumers. However, sometimes these static rates are the best price in the market and sometimes they're not, as we know. To mitigate the issue of having uncompetitive rates, said travel agent might also start working with online travel agents to access OTA contracted dynamic rates. Perhaps the OTA shares a bit of the commission they receive from the hotel to the traditional travel agent. Perhaps the traditional travel agent (we'll call them a wholesaler) also shares their static contracted rates with the OTA, so the OTA also has access to lower rates they can mark up and sell as well. Do you see how this could get very confusing very quickly? There's no way to know if the price you see for a room on an OTA site is one that you've given them, or one that you've given a wholesaler who has in turn shared it with the OTA. Unless you make a booking on the OTA's site and see what source it comes in from in your property management system (either the OTA or the wholesaler) it is exceedingly difficult to determine.

And so begins the complexity of distribution, which is why it's impossible to easily demonstrate who goes where and why in a diagram.

Why It Matters

What I can tell you is it's very, very important to pick a set of market and channel categories that are relevant for your hotel (or group of hotels) and try as best you can to accurately label each reservation made with the appropriate market/channel.

Why? Because data is powerful.

> *When you can look at the big picture of who is staying at your hotel and why, you can focus your efforts on each source individually.*

Not understanding your market or channel segments would be like promoting your hotel on a giant billboard nearby and hoping everyone sitting in their homes will somehow see it. Your advertising spend on it would have been futile. If, however, you know a large percentage of your business books your hotel online, then you can focus your efforts on *digital* marketing, like buying relevant Google search terms like 'boutique hotels in [your] city' for example. It lets you see and say, 'our OTA business is down, let's see if we can participate in a promotion or marketing campaign they might have, we need the help next month', and then action accordingly.

I'm sure you have a general idea of what segments to choose for your hotel, and keep in mind that if you do make a change, it will take a full 365 days before you can start to truly look at year-over-year comparisons. You'll have to get by with piecing together old data with new data and possibly comparing apples to oranges until then. Or if fruit isn't your thing, you can always enlist the help of a consultant to conduct a health check of your data and suggest how it can be sorted. Better data will improve and streamline your marketing efforts for each channel and market segment.

> The most important part is that you categorise your distribution channels in ways that are tangible enough to impact their performance with bespoke tactics when needed.

Segmentation

I wish I could offer a golden set of segments, but each hotel or group of hotels will differ slightly. In my experience, the most accurate way to segment is when both channel *and* market segments are included on your reservations and can be extracted into your database for reporting purposes. Generally, sub-segmenting the markets into the following three categories will assist to more easily identify what books best and help to generate more of it:

- BAR Rates: *What comes in under your 'regular' rate (hotels might call it Best Available Rate [BAR] or Rack).*
- Discounted Rates: *What books in under discounted pricing (long-standing discounted offers that almost always are available, such as 'early bird' or 'stay 3 nights, pay only 2 nights' for example).*
- Promotional Rates: *Temporary or seasonal promotions, offers, packages, that switch 'on' and 'off' more frequently.*

This allows you to easily see and manipulate the various efforts you're making in each sub-segment to meet your revenue goals. It also allows you to strategize pricing to achieve your ADR. If, for example, you notice that most of your reservations are booked on discounted rates (the ones you make available almost permanently), then you may decide to increase your BAR rate pricing, which in turn will lift your discounted price points as well. Shutting off the discount rates might completely shut off the customers who are only willing to book if they feel they're getting a good deal and would never pay full price (my mother, for example). Tracking your production in ways relevant to your hotel will allow for more accurate insights and the ability to create optimal tactics that maximize revenue.

Control Your Inventory

This is where it gets a little more confusing. We're going to skip over a 'how it's distributed' talk, because every hotel and business will use different systems, software and methods. Instead, we'll jump straight into an important lesson about being in full control of your product. Allow me to explain.

Your revenue or distribution manager, or whomever is responsible for changing prices and managing rate plans at your property, will be offered by many a distributor to setup rate plans, promotions, even inventory, *for them*.

For example, you'd like to participate in a sale Expedia is having where the hotel will be included in a 'Save 30% on hotels in [your] city!' promotion. There are usually two setup options:
- Either the hotel team creates the rate plan in the property management system (PMS) and takes the relevant steps to link this rate plan to Expedia, typically via a Channel Management System, or
- Expedia will offer to take this job off your plate and *create it in their system* for you instead (as would every other third-party distributor that you work with most likely).

You're grateful for the help and take option two (because, outsourcing, right?).

The offer is on sale for three days only, and everything is going well—bookings are being made, revenue is being generated, and you're managing pricing based on the demand accordingly.

Here's where it starts to get dubious....

After the agreed three days, you notice 30% off rates are still trickling in from the OTA, in fact for days and days you keep seeing them dropping into your system. You look in your PMS and see that you have the 30% rate plan closed out, so how are they still coming through? Simple. Because you delegated this *to your distributor*, who realizing they have a very attractive rate for your hotel and your market, may have 'accidentally' forgotten to shut down the offer at the end of the sale period. "Oops," they say, and close it as soon as you address it with them.

Look, I'm not accusing anyone of being anything but upright in their business, particularly distributors who are promoting an endless number of different sales and hotels at any one time, it's a lot to keep track of. However, I will say that in the case of third parties, they know it's in their best interest to have the most attractive rate in the market. They also work with a lot of hotels, manage a lot of platforms, offers, promotions, and countries. It's only human if they legitimately forget to switch one off on time which is why you're better off controlling it yourself.

Despite what you might think, I'm not trying to blame or point fingers at anyone, I'm simply saying do your best *to control your inventory yourself.* It won't always be possible. You may want or need to have a distributor prepay for rooms for your own cash flow purposes, options like this do exist at times. Just know that if, and when, you hand over any amount of your product to a third party to sell, it becomes *their product to sell however they please.*

For example, say a florist located next to my café enlisted my help to sell her bouquets to my customers. She has a high amount of perishable inventory and knows if she doesn't sell them all, the flowers will eventually wilt and be unsellable. So she approaches me and asks if I'll buy their bouquets for $10 apiece, explaining that they retail for $30, so I'll be profiting $20 per bunch I sell. Wonderful, I say, and buy ten.

Now I'm selling flowers for $30, just like the florist is, same flowers, same price, different purchase points. I look over at the flower shop and see lots of bouquets being sold, but no one is buying mine. I start to worry that I just put out $100 in cost of flowers for zero income. So I reduce the price of mine to $20 each. I sell them all, and I profit $100 from the sales. What this has done in the meantime, however, is halt bouquet sales at the florist. Everyone is buying from me instead, as I've got the same bouquets but for $10 less, right next door. The florist isn't happy, but they know there isn't much they can do because I paid for those bunches upfront and could therefore do with them as I pleased. I could have charged $50 each instead or giving them away for free to my loyal customers. In other words, when you buy lemons from the grocery store, the shop can't tell you to only use them for lemonade – you've paid for them upfront, you can do with them as you please. It's the same concept.

Rate Parity

The discussion of rate parity comes front and centre when a business is no longer in strong control of their inventory. I urge you to remember this when you see lower prices displayed for your product elsewhere. Before you start demanding they sell at a certain price, or mark up by a certain amount, think about how they got your inventory first. If they bought it from you outright, so to speak, you cannot tell them what or how to price your product to their customers. However, if they are simply acting as an agent and receive a commission once the product is sold, then a pre-determined retail price *can* be set.

In the florist example, if the owner had come over to tell me that I *must* price the flowers at $30 each, that would be considered 'price fixing'. Why? Because the florist has a shop front, and so do

I at my café, which makes us competitors. The flower shop is the supplier, true, but because they sell publicly, they're also a retailer, and one competitor cannot tell another competitor how to price. If they had said they would pay me a $20 commission every time I sold a bouquet, this would have meant two things. First, that I wouldn't have paid anything out of pocket to have their flowers in my cafe. If I didn't sell any, the florist would simply take them all back. Second, if I did sell all ten, I would owe them $300 of the monies I'd collected from the purchases, and the florist in turn would give me $200 in commission.

In summary, hotels distribute rooms and room rates to a wide variety of travel agents (both online and offline), to wholesale companies, tour operators, businesses and various organisations. These distribution partners use a multitude of business to business (B to B) and business to consumer (B to C) websites and channels to on-sell hotel room pricing to the end consumer. Ideally, you want the partner selling at the same rate as the hotel, or higher. In fact, you ideally only want lower rates to ever be publicly found on your own website, not a third party one. One way to mitigate the repercussions of lower rates through third party distribution partners is by having a 'Best Rate Guarantee' policy, which allows consumers to feel confident they always will, or always can, get the best and lowest price by booking directly through hotel-owned channels directly.

As best they can, hotels should not enter into any agreements that insist on price parity—it's a recipe for disaster and a race to the bottom (i.e., who will try to sell at the lowest rate to win the business). We, as hoteliers, want to be able to sell our product for whatever price we deem appropriate, because it's *our* product. We want third party agents to sell at what they've agreed to mark up by (but again, not a specific price point) and wholesalers to bundle their rate in a tour package or the like to ensure their rate stays opaque, because those are the rates we've determined we need in order to achieve our overall revenue goals.

> *No one should be telling anyone else how to price the available product that they have, and especially those entities considered to be in competition with one another.*

It's a very grey area with very murky waters, and several companies have gotten into trouble for this in the past. Tread carefully, seek legal advice, and work with fair trade bodies in your industry to ensure you are being compliant and obeying consumer law. Look up the word 'collusion' if you'd like to learn more.

Why It Matters

Hotels are constantly badgered by distributors they've engaged with, sold rooms to, or have agreed could act as an agent and sell on their behalf. They want to have their cake and eat it too, who doesn't. Say you've given an agent a dynamic rate with a 10% commission, this means they're on-selling price to their customers that's identical to yours, and very adaptable to your hotel's (and the market's) conditions. It's the most relevant rate, but not always as low as the wholesale ones.

However, agents with dynamic rates want you to give them static rates too. That way, if your dynamic rates are higher than your static wholesale prices, they can jump over to the cheaper fixed rates and sell those instead. Having a static rate means that in theory it should be lower than your dynamic prices, however there's a probability that it could be higher, as we learned in the previous chapter. Because you established them a year in advance, maybe more, they likely were set very conservatively, and rightfully so. No crystal ball is that accurate yet.

The problem is, unless your website, or your property management system, can also sell both dynamic and static simultaneously, giving any one agent both types of rates means you start to have a rate discrepancy problem. Your distributors are now advertising a lower rate than your own hotel, creating a disloyalty with your customers who may start to think you're somehow penalizing them, despite being faithful and booking directly on your site. It's also propelling your hotel into cyberspace chaos on the World Wide Web. You'll start finding your hotel's prices on random websites that you've never heard of, let alone work with, because agents on-sell to other agents, and wholesalers will on-sell to other wholesalers in order to move inventory faster and generate more revenue for themselves through higher volumes at smaller mark-ups or margins.

I'd wager that most Revenue Managers would nod in agreement when I confess that I've spent way, way too much time playing detective, trying to determine which of our contracted distributors was giving rogue third party sites our inventory. Being displayed and sold far and wide is not the issue. The problem is that most of these on-selling sites don't mark up their prices high enough to be in parity with our own. That means they'll show prices, from a few dollars to a few hundred, less than those on our sites. Again, that's not the end of the world, but if you have a Best Rate Guarantee policy (which you should) it means you're processing claims, giving guests discounts, and chasing your tail trying to figure out how to get the rate fixed or removed on the rogue site every time. It's endless, and exhausting.

You'll also become a mediator for all the agents you work with who are seeing different rates to what they each have. Suddenly, the companies you used to see as allies in selling your rooms start behaving like children fighting over toys. Expedia will want to know why Booking.com has a lower price than they do. You might realise that Booking.com has contracted with one of your wholesalers and is receiving the static prices, which explains the variance. Expedia doesn't care about the reason—they just want the price. And you don't care about the price, you want to fix the reason, not give them the lower price too.

Are you confused yet? You're not alone if you are, I often am too. Seek out a revenue expert or sales manager with wholesale expertise, and spend some time getting to know how all the players in your hotel's distribution world work, it's important.

Do your best to control your hotel's inventory.

That means when it comes to your product, be very deliberate about who you contract with, who you sell to, and what terms you put around what they can and cannot do with what you give. Can they on-sell to third party agents? If you don't want them to, say so, and make sure it's in writing. They still might do it, but when you shut down their room supply entirely because of it, I assure you they'll be quick to rectify the problem.

Complications

The more complicated you make it, the messier it gets. And maybe that's okay for your hotel, maybe you don't care so much about who and how people book, you just want 'heads in beds' to fill your rooms and maximise revenue. And that's completely fine, however I'd venture to say that one day when you are satisfied with the revenue coming in yet scratching your head on all the costs going out, some of them will be distribution related, be it commissions, or channels, mark-ups, margins or discounts. You'll start to wonder if you could reduce some of those expenses and make more profit, and how it can be done. You'll realise that if you start relying less on the high commission distributors and more on the lower cost ones (including your own website, walk-ins, and telephone reservations), you'll squeeze out more juice to the bottom line. Inevitably, you'll begin to review the terms of your contracts, who you want to stop working with, who you want to re-negotiate with, and spend long hours mapping it out. And yes, this is all part of doing business with third parties. But keep in mind that it's best not to tarnish relationship when preventable. Meaning, if you don't complicate it in the first place, you won't need to have the uncomfortable conversations down the line.

The world of hotel distribution is incestuous. Everyone is obtaining inventory from everyone else in a bid to have it all and be able to display the best price and win a piece of the business—*your business*—your hotel rooms.

> *If nothing else, remember that it's your inventory, they are all just middlemen helping you sell it.*

I'm not diminishing the value of distributing your rooms through the aid of others, quite the opposite. I'm simply saying that these middlemen should each be providing value that you yourself would have difficulty affording otherwise. Ideally, the reach of each one should be unique. For example, EVENT Hospitality is one of the largest hotel companies in Australia, and during my years with them prior to COVID-19, most of their guests were domestic travellers. A lot of Australians knew the Rydges, QT, Thredbo, and Atura branded hotels without needing an OTA to tell them what they were, or what to expect. This meant their hotels generated a higher-than-average percentage of bookings via their respective branded websites, in some cases more than OTAs. Their domestic bookings were solid, and they didn't need OTAs intervening on their local business by trying to convert domestic guests to book via the OTA website when they were already doing so on each hotel's own.

They did, however, need help in the international arena. I know that's almost a laughable scenario in 2021, but we'll get back there again someday, humour me for now. Few people globally had heard of their brands beyond New Zealand and wouldn't have had the faintest inclination of going directly to the hotel's website when they hardly even knew the brand's name. This is where OTAs with global presence, Booking.com for example, would help by displaying the QT's and Rydges side-by-side against big international hotel chain options, making these domestic hotels a viable consideration for international customers to contemplate as well. Originally, Booking.com and Expedia provided access to different markets. Both players emerged in 1996, however Booking.com hailing from Holland gave it a strong European presence while Expedia's Washington roots dominated North America. Had the lines never blurred and connectivity never emerged, this would have been the ideal example of leveraging different companies to reach different markets.

Hotels were grateful for each OTA's broader reach and vast platforms because it would otherwise cost millions to reach these overseas audiences themselves. Hotels, and businesses in general, gladly pay a commission for sales third parties generate from the greater globe that they couldn't reach, be it language barriers or affordability, and wouldn't have otherwise obtained. Distributors should be able to demonstrate their unique reach when pitching to hotels, so that the hotel in turn can fully understand and support having them as a distributor. If a product owner can truly comprehend the value they're getting for the costs (commission or otherwise), the relationship will be easy, straightforward, and mutually beneficial.

Distribution is complex, complicated and highly beneficial for increasing top-line revenues when fully understood and leveraged properly. I urge everyone to do a bit more digging into distribution, or the equivalent for your industry. Hire a consultant to do a deep-dive and explain it specifically as it relates to your hotel without bias. Otherwise, have a chat with your sales or revenue manager who is responsible for these relationships at your property, and they'll surely map it out for you.

> *Keep it simple, know where you're selling your rooms and why.*

Control

When you are the owner of a product, it's important to remember that you are in full control. You decide when, where, how, and who to sell it to. You decide even if you want to sell it. Not everything about your business is in your control of course, moving parts will fail from time to time, but being both the provider and a distributer gives you an advantage over your third-party resellers. They are all just passengers, *you* are the driver. You get to decide where to go.

Above all else, place your hotel's website higher than all others in your mind. Whether or not it's a less or more expensive way of distribution for your establishment is irrelevant because it's one of the most loyalty driven ways for guests to book a room, and loyalty is paramount. People coming to your site means *they chose you*, and they didn't need to shop around on an OTA and check out what other hotels were available, because they already *knew* they wanted to stay with you. Cherish that loyalty, and honour it as much as you can, be it with discounted rates, better service, perks or amenities.

Loyal guests create a cult-like following who'll brag about their stay, praise you in online reviews and social media and suggest you for their travel requirements in future. Think about the companies, stores and brands you're most loyal to and why. Work out the *why*. Remember to stay *most loyal* to your hotel, its integrity, and who you give the permission and privilege of selling your rooms and representing your brand to.

7

LOYALTY

Loyalty is by far the most cost-effective way to drive revenue and enhance the reputation of your hotel.

Loyalty, like revenue, is universal. It doesn't require a program, a membership or a stated reason, being loyal to a brand is based on the feeling it evokes for you. In the United States, millions of people are loyally, undyingly and everlastingly devoted to Disney. And not just to Disney per se, but either to Disneyland *or* Disney World, never usually both, always just one. And the insult you elicit to someone when you mistake their loyalty for the *wrong* one? For the number of times I've mistakenly referenced Disney World instead of Disneyland to one of my best friends and die-hard fan, Jessica, I'm amazed she still puts up with me. "Clearly there's a big difference!" she'd say as she corrected me. Disneyland sparks a special feeling of joy for her beyond the logic of the brand. Disneyworld does not. Noted, Jess.

Loyalty is the reason *beyond* the surface reason that people go out of their way to buy a certain product. A shoe is a shoe, but a Nike shoe for me is the only way to go when it comes to athletic footwear. Coke and Pepsi are both brown liquids with heaps of sugar and splashes of caffeine, but I wouldn't touch a Pepsi unless it was life or death. Like it or not, we all have devotions to certain things. More often than not, the reason is solely because of the feeling it conjures, not the flavour but rather an emotion, a core life principle that it satisfies for us. It might be a product, a sports team, country, show, person, brand, or even an app, loyalty knows no bounds.

> *Loyalty goes beyond points, status and membership, because at its core is the way it makes you feel—understood and special.*

When I first went to Singapore with my husband and our little boys, we had no idea where to stay or what hotel to choose. Every friend had an opinion or a past experience they wanted to impart, but there were so many that it became overwhelming. So, like many, we read the hotel reviews online, picked one that was within our price range, and took a risk. We decided on the Four Seasons hotel, despite it being situated closer towards the government and business district. Worrying that perhaps it would not align for a family with two small children, in the end we chose it because we had never stayed at a Four Seasons before, and it was surprisingly affordable compared to other Singapore options. That said, we were also aware this 'affordability' was because it would be undergoing room renovations during our stay. It was situated within walking distance of Orchard Street and all the shops, and though our expectations of enjoying a hotel under construction were low, we were hopeful our first stay at a Four Seasons would be nice nonetheless.

When we arrived, a car was waiting with juice boxes that had each child's name printed on a sticker underneath the hotel logo. We sat on plush sofas in the lobby while we were comfortably checked in by one staff member, and then escorted to our room by the same associate. As she walked us through each room feature, I noticed see there was already a cot for the baby, as requested, along with two tissue wrapped nappies and a small set of baby bath soaps and lotions. It was so thoughtful. When I opened the closet, I noticed standard hotel items, a safe, an iron, luggage rack and hangers, however next to the adult bathrobes hung a miniature child size one, with a small set of bath slippers below. The construction noise turned out to be a non-issue as it was many floors below, and the service and thoughtfulness well exceeded our expectations. Now every time we visit Singapore, we stay in that hotel without a second thought. When you boil it down, the cost of our loyalty to the hotel was two nappies, a few dollars for baby bath amenities, and kindness from the staff.

Loyalty is a satisfaction, not a material possession.

Hotels have long been refining their loyalty programs, just like airlines. OTAs have also cottoned on to creating them, but at the end of the day, they can only reward a customer for *how* they book, they don't have actual hotels to further the service experience. Unless a hotel agrees to offer preferential treatment on their behalf, the OTA is powerless to reward loyalty at a hotel level.

Which brings us to our first point in creating a program for your hotel.

You must define what it is you want guests to be loyal to before you determine how to incentivise them.

For example, if you want them to be dedicated to booking via your hotel's proprietary website, or directly at the hotel, you'll need to create rewards around *how* or where they book their stay. If you just want them to be loyal to your hotel, full stop, you're not so bothered about how they book so long as they choose you above the competitors, then you'll be looking to reward customers with benefits for simply *staying* with you, regardless of how they made their reservation. With this type of recognition, you'll treat everyone who stays with an equal level of gratitude for their business, regardless of how they booked their visit.

Once you've decided what you want to encourage loyalty for (*how* they book or *what hotel* they choose), you can start forming a program that rewards guests accordingly. If it's booking via your website (the *how*), perhaps you offer them an exclusive member discount for making their reservation via your URL. You might provide more relaxed policies for them, like easier cancellations or more flexibility with date changes, refunds, etc. There could also be a tiered system in play, however it strictly only rewards based on the nights stayed that are booked a certain way, which can become frustrating to members, as I'll explain.

Sometimes we assume guests know the difference between *how* and *what* they book, yet I'm convinced these are operational terms, and not part of a guest's vocabulary. There's also the business travel component that influences one's booking method. Some people might be booking on your hotel's website for a personal stay, but have a company policy to make a reservation via their contracted TMC when they travel for business. Or perhaps a conference has a block of rooms and requires attendees to book via their external meeting coordinator instead of directly through the hotel. Often these stays aren't recognised by rewards programs, and often these guests are confused.

Whether you entice loyalty for your brand or for a booking method, the program might be tiered based on the number of nights guests stay with you. If rewarding a booking method, then you're only counting the number of nights stayed that specifically booked via your website or at the hotel. This perhaps is achieved by using the tiered levels of membership, unlocking upgraded amenities, a complimentary cocktail, spa use, late checkout, or a combination thereof the more frequently they stay.

There's no right answer here. It will take a lot of discussion, market research, guest polling, and analysing of other companies and industries. Developing a deep understanding of your brand's presence in the market, the organic demand it attracts and what boost you believe the business needs to increase that demand. Some hotels don't have a loyalty program at all! Some don't belong to a network, affiliation program, hotel chain, franchise, or anything—and they still thrive. Loyalty programs with points and tiers aren't always the answer, but you won't determine what's right for your hotel until you take a very holistic approach to defining what you want and need for your property.

Bigger Fish in the Pond

There's also the fundamental truth that loyalty programs for the travel industry perform better when they're on a national and/or global scale. Your singular hotel, creating a singular program, will not likely move the dial significantly enough to see a positive result. This doesn't mean you shouldn't recognize and reward loyalty, quite the contrary, but you don't need a member number to do that, you just need to internally decide how you'd like to acknowledge different behaviours and frequencies of stay. Mr. Money may visit you so often that every 100th night you offer him something extra special. Mrs. Moderation on the other hand might stay less often, but she's a routine regular every year and is worthy of recognition, perhaps a welcome amenity and a personal card from the hotel manager.

Most of the time, loyalty is created when people feel seen and are recognized, and that's it.

Think of your favourite coffee shop—is it the coffee? Or the smile, and the fact they remember your name? Your favourite airline—is it the quality of the aircraft (hint, many are made by Boeing, and are the same product except for the different fit-out and colours) or the service and recognition you're given? Sometimes membership is a hassle for customers, such as small businesses who offer a stamp card with a discount or free item after ten purchases. Nice in theory, but with smart phones as wallets these days, remembering to carry around a punch-card to save a few dollars isn't worth the hassle.

I stopped automatically scanning my membership numbers at a few major grocery stores because I couldn't easily recognise what the benefit of doing so was giving me. Providing my details with each purchase was giving the store lots of analytics about my buying behaviour, but for me the rewards were too vague to waste extra time while checking out. I stopped being loyal 'to a fault', particularly because the fault was just a default I'd become accustomed to doing. However, when the cashier asked me about redeeming a $10 credit I had, I started scanning my card again.

Loyalty programs should be fun, simple, inspiring and motivating for customers to love you more. They don't have to be the same as your competitor or even similar, and they don't need to be overly complex. The most important aspect of anything you do in the interest of your guests is to find out *what they want* before you get started, not what *you think* they want. Maybe your program rewards what they buy, or how they book, maybe a little bit of both. The key to remember is service. Ensure everyone is on the same page as far as the priorities of rewarding behaviours are concerned. Doing so means no one, not the guest or the employee, gets upset or confused. Crystal clear objectives, vision, and rewards—don't reinvent the wheel. Hindsight is 20/20, use history's trials and errors to your advantage. Research the methods that exist and those that came and went, then make something that works easily for you and the service you're providing.

We touched on this earlier, but again, how do we know what people really want? Of course, everyone is different, and they all want different things, but, people want to feel valued, understood and like they matter to you, that they are special. They might be satisfied with nothing more than an amicable arrival experience, or it might involve more pomp and circumstance, a room upgrade, for example. There are two easy ways to get a better idea of what customers want—read reviews and be a lobby lizard.

Read Reviews

Customers only tend to write a review when they are overly thrilled, overly upset, or being given a reward for writing a comment. Most of the time you'll be able to decipher from the three. Jump onto review platforms, there are countless sites these days, and thankfully several companies that collate them all together for you. Read everything, and make sure you have someone at your hotel dedicated to posting prompt and sincere replies to ensure your guests feel valued for taking the time to give feedback. Start to see the common threads of good and bad and how you can change, improve or capitalize on them. Don't stop with your hotel either—is there a competitor you want to emulate? Read their reviews and find out what they're doing well. What are they doing poorly? How can you use their negatives as a positive selling feature for your future clients and guests?

Be a Lobby Lizard

I don't know who coined that phrase or why, but essentially it means hang out in your lobby and greet guests passing by. Ask them about their stay, chit chat, make them feel special. Ask them how they booked, why they booked, buy them a coffee, give them a handshake, whatever it takes for them to feel valued and not inconvenienced. It sounds like a lot, but standing in the lobby for thirty minutes, a few days a week, could make all the difference, it might soothe guests' agitation of waiting in line to check in or out, or puff the chests of those needing external recognition when they converse with upper management.

I once worked with a General Manager who started asking his guests how they booked their room. If they hadn't booked directly on the hotel website, he would gently prompt them to explain why. The fascinating answer he received once from a guest who said they'd booked via Booking.com, was something along the lines of, "But I *did* book on your site, I went online and booked, and here I am, I booked your hotel on Booking.com."

Which leads us to the next point—don't assume.

Don't Assume

Have you heard what the word 'assume' stands for? When you assume, it makes an ASS out of U and ME. ASS.U.ME. It has never done me any good to think I know what people want without finding out first. In corporate office meetings I was often compelled to remind our team of leaders, who would boast that they knew how hotel teams really operate and what guests genuinely think, that as executives in a corporate office, we don't. Sitting in a meeting room on a high floor in a beautiful building in the centre of Sydney—we did not in fact know anything about the inner workings of each hotel, exactly as they were operating *right then, in that moment*. It's a bit like a parent thinking they know precisely what their teenager is doing all the time (did you always tell mum and dad what you were up to?) Even if you did, there are always a lot of assumptions being made. As executives we couldn't know everything, unless we were in the hotel with them, finding out firsthand.

Hotels teams will often tell the company's executives what they *think* they want to hear. They will do what they've been asked without mentioning the undue strain it's causing. I know this because I was guilty of it in my early hotel days when the all-important VIP corporate office team would come to visit. It's natural to want to impress, showcase the capabilities and competencies of your team and their abilities, especially to the big, big bosses. Yet at the end of the day, honesty really is the best policy. It's not realistic to ASSUME anything, not of your guests or the wants of your superiors, unless open discussions or proper research have taken place. Sometimes we give so much credit to people, when in reality they have no idea. We think (or assume) they must surely know something as extensively as we do when actually they do not, and vice versa.

A few years ago, I had a revelation. As an industry, we were always wanting guests to 'book direct' and in turn we'd reward their loyalty. Not wanting them booking on third parties, we would shout, "Book direct and save!" from every platform possible. We'd say, "Become a [loyalty program] member and get [XYZ] benefits!"

> *One day it occurred to me that, as hoteliers, we know what it means to book direct, and that our membership program is free—but do our guests? Or do we need to take a step back and educate our audience on what these mean?*

It's time to drop the hotel jargon.

That guest questioned in the lobby sincerely thought he was booking 'direct'. He went on a website, made a booking, and there he was, staying at the hotel he chose. "Is that not direct?" he might wonder? Likewise, with a loyalty program—some companies still charge membership fees, so are we deterring sign-ups by not emphasizing when it's complimentary? Do we need to be clearer about it if it always was and always will be free, no strings attached? "We just need your email address to sign you up and send you great offers. Oh, and did we mention it's free?"

Read your audience, this includes colleagues, partners, children or otherwise. Listen and engage, never assume, and as in life, everyone will be better for it.

Guest Complaints

Sometimes the best feedback is provided by what's not said.

A mediocre stay probably won't warrant a customer review. It takes time and effort to write something or give feedback, and if all was 'just okay' what's the point? Understanding what *isn't* being said is just as important as what is. Asking guests how their stay was, inviting them to provide feedback without judgment, is what converts someone from 'maybe' to 'definitely' will try you again sometime. If they really loved their stay or hated it, they'll be very inclined to let you know, either in person, via email, or online. A 'so-so' experience typically will not, unless they feel strongly about a certain aspect, or that they didn't receive value for their money, for example.

In my Starwood Hotels days (now part of the Marriott family) I was a Service Culture Trainer at the Westin in Las Vegas, in addition to my revenue role. Every month or so, another trainer and I, very often it was my Disneyland obsessed friend Jessica, would spend a day with the team, training them on what it meant to be part of the Starwood family. Sometimes it was new hires, sometimes existing employees due for a refresher. We'd talk about loyalty and the cult-like following that certain brands elicit, about customer retention and ideas on how to do it—such as giving a 'surprise or delight' in some fashion that the guest didn't expect. We'd drill down into the service recovery process, and the challenge of converting a hater into a lover of your company—the sweet spot, and the victory.

Service recovery is serious business for any organisation. If you can understand the real problem and compensate accordingly, you just may create a customer for life. Guests want to be heard and understood, which means throwing a stock standard compensation policy at everyone won't work, it might in fact even offend them beyond repair. This also goes for responding to online reviews. If a company's response is a cookie-cutter copy/paste for each person's feedback, it is most certainly perceived as insincere and dismissive. Not only does the review author feel a sense of frustration and betrayal, but so too do the people researching reviews, and the management's responses, as part of their decision-making process to book their hotel.

> *Understanding why the guest is upset, repeating their concerns back to them so they know you understand, then asking what you can do to help make things better is the best recipe to recover a guest's satisfaction.*

You'd be amazed at what some people want! In Las Vegas, I'd get the most irate complaints, usually well justified, by guests fuming about their mistreatment. Reasons ranging from their room not being ready when they arrived, being placed in a smoking room when they preferred non, to neighbouring guests being too noisy, the list was endless. During each encounter, I'd mentally brace myself for what I would, or could, compensate with to make things better, generally thinking a partial refund or hotel credit would be necessary for the big ones. Dollars usually worked—some guests warmed to the idea of a food and beverage credit to enjoy dinner in the hotel, while others expected a discount off their room rate.

Ironically, it seemed that the guests who were most visibly upset usually wanted compensation that was lower in cost to the hotel than I was prepared to offer. I'd hear huffs and puffs of upset and criticisms, I knew it wasn't all *our* fault, a delayed flight can make a hotel check-in experience feel so much longer than it is, for example. While I knew guests wouldn't necessarily acknowledge the external stack of events in their day that contributed to channelling their dissatisfaction towards our hotel, I also knew this was my chance to turn their day around. As they stood at my desk, some flaunting their membership status or self-proclaimed loyalty, expressing the sheer regret of their decision to choose our hotel instead of one of the many others in town, I would hear, acknowledge and apologise for their inconveniences. Then I would ask if there was anything I could possibly do to make the situation better.

Those squeaky wheels were often the ones who needed the least amount of grease. Sometimes they just wanted a late checkout to compensate for their issues. Realising what they *really* wanted was simply to be heard, I always offered my gratitude for their feedback and would raise their concerns with the relevant departments of our hotel. After all, if the team didn't know, how could they evolve and grow? Each complaint was firsthand feedback on how we could improve, our very own in-house market research system. If the guest's request was seemingly small, I would honour it without hesitation, then excitedly brainstorm ways to surprise and delight them with something extra, something creative that helped reinforce that they were indeed heard and valued. Sometimes it was a VIP turndown service in their room if the complaint was related to housekeeping. The in-room movies back then were pay-per-view, easily problematic when they weren't working while the guest was still being charged, but also easily fixable with an extra movie credit or for a few complimentary items from the mini bar.

Such instances were always an opportunity to surprise and delight in some way. If a guest had been inconvenienced because their room wasn't ready in time for their anniversary dinner, I could send them to get ready in the spa's facilities and promise to put their luggage in their room as soon as it was ready while they were out. Later, I'd send up a cheese platter, with a note apologizing again for the inconvenience and wishing them an enjoyable rest of their stay and anniversary. The gift of giving is always a joy, especially when the recipient appreciates the thoughtfulness, regardless of its value.

I once met a guest who was attending a black-tie event and needed someone to sew the tear on his tuxedo pants pocket. I remember explaining that because it was late, housekeeping had already gone home, but I would see what I could do to help. He was very understanding and asked me for a black Sharpie (Texta), saying he could probably colour the white inner pocket lining with black and no one would notice the tear. I thought it was funny, but he was serious. I took the pair of trousers, sewed the seam as best I could (it wasn't awful, but I'm no professional) and sent them up to his room. I also included an envelope containing a black Sharpie and a note that said, "Just in case." He was so grateful for the hotel going above and beyond the call of duty, and it just took a few minutes and a few dollars for a Texta. He left glowing reviews about our team online, and on our hotel satisfaction surveys too. Cost little, loyalty high.

> *The ideas for compensation are endless, but not always easy to execute at every hotel. A great idea is to come up with a few good ones that will both work for your operations team and satisfy your guests.*

It provides your employees with a confidence-boosting toolkit knowing what they have at the ready to offer when appropriate. Creating framework and boundaries with your team about costs and what is or is not appropriate will help empower them to solve problems autonomously, saving both their manager's and the customer's time. The more a team understands how to read people's emotions, the easier it is to navigate complaints in the face of confrontation. Sometimes something as simple as a late check-out is the answer—costs you nothing, but means everything to the guest who needs to feel respected and understood.

Loyalty in Customer Service

Furthering my point about autonomy, it's important with service recovery, and with loyalty, that *all* your teams are empowered with a set of tools they can use without needing permission. You might give your reservations agents the ability to discount, upgrade, or honour lower rates found elsewhere to retain a call or book their business. You may tell your front desk they can offer food and beverage vouchers of a certain dollar amount, a room upgrade, send specified room service amenities, or discount/credit a room charge up to a certain amount. They are now equipped to deal with confrontation in the moment instead of waiting for approval.

> *Quality customer service is pivotal. Not just for loyalty, but for the ability to command stronger room rates too.*

I hardly remember what room rate I paid on our second visit to Singapore because it was within reason of other hotels, and I knew the Four Seasons was where I wanted to stay. When customer service is the culture in your business it's easy to retain *and* obtain even more, regardless of what type of product you have. Certainly, there are also obvious factors, as your reviews will indicate, some in and some out of your control. Cleanliness, for example, is a key component, but if you can master that basic need and excel at service, you'll be surprised at what other issues guests are willing to look past.

Marketing & PR

You might wonder why I've included marketing and public relations (PR) in a chapter about loyalty. Truth is, they do contribute to influencing consumers to choose your brand. As a revenue person, you might have already guessed I'm not the biggest advocate of marketing or PR, because as a numbers person I know there's no truly accurate way to tell if the money, time, and effort have any direct correlation to the revenue coming in. Sure, there are metrics and analytics, how else would these departments justify their efforts? They create a plausible Return on Investment (ROI), indicating that their spend has been worthwhile by way of revenue generated as a result of their efforts. These two departments are a bit like vitamins—you don't know if you need to take them, or if you even notice a difference when you do, but research says they're good for you, so you consume them anyway, hope they help, and give benefit of the doubt. Whether or not they've changed your body for the better is difficult to determine, but overall you're feeling pretty good, might as well keep taking them.

I'd venture to say that in a similar manner to taking supplements, when it comes to marketing and PR, research says they are good for you—in moderation and when affordable, so you might as well partake when you can. There's no doubt brand recognition is paramount in the grand scheme of things, but as hoteliers, we never really know if the marketing efforts made all the difference, or whether that super sharp promotional rate that was made available along with it would have garnered the same revenue results on its own.

Buying keywords on search engines such as Google is a clearer way to see if what you're spending is paying off, but it's not entirely accurate either. It helps you determine what buzz words your buyers are persuaded by, for example, 'best hotels near Queen Victoria Building in Sydney'. That could be a good key phrase to attract bookings for QT Sydney if it's something that people commonly search for since it's just around the corner. The hotel can then see how many viewers clicked, how many then booked, and whether the cost of buying the key phrase was worthwhile when compared with what came in as revenue, the ROI.

There's no question that the better and more prominently you see brands advertised, the more they seep into your subconscious.

Next time you want to buy a nice piece of jewellery, you might be inexplicably drawn to visit Tiffany & Co. Perhaps you'd plausibly deny that all the poster ads at the bus stops where you commute, the first page magazine spreads, or the celebrities showcasing their treasures at award shows, don't all add up to one idea that you should visit Tiffany's. You might credit your sense of taste or confess that you were inspired by the ads or PR placement of jewels on celebrities, but really the reason doesn't matter. If they got you through the door, and even better got you to make a purchase, their efforts at eliciting a positive emotion towards their brand were achieved, mission accomplished. As long as the business remains profitable, despite their high advertising costs, then they don't need to know the exact bus stop or celebrity that was the catalyst for you. Instead they can be content that their formula is working and can keep the mix of marketing mediums they use. If the advertising spend compared to the revenue growth is agreeable for a healthy profit, it implies they should keep going with a good thing.

Outsourcing Loyalty

Yes, marketing is important, and arguably healthy, so long as you don't overdose on too many 'vitamins'. Positive PR is great when you can get it. There are many good reasons to consider becoming part of a branded hotel chain, and these are certainly some of them. Bigger brands are vested in more than just the interest of your hotel, but for the greater good of their label at large, which is always to your benefit. It saves you time and money by way of not having to determine who, what, where and how to spend your dollars and maximise your presence independently. Hotel groups afford high-level talent that provide expert guidance and higher bang for your buck than doing it all yourself. Leveraging the strength in numbers allows an independent hotel to ride the coattails of a higher profile brand, while still reaping the benefits of being an individually owned hotel. It includes your business in a portfolio of an already well-loved brand of hotels, while still allowing a level of owner control and autonomy.

Joining forces with an existing group of hotels also allows your hotel to plug right into an up and running loyalty program, or database of loyal subscribers at the very least. Other benefits include larger presence and buying power that comes from outsourcing loyalty by entering a collaborative arrangement. Opting into a management agreement, alliance, collective, or association of some sort is worth thoughtful consideration as it can help increase brand awareness and level up your loyalty.

Commerce

> *Loyalty, in the commerce world, ultimately distils down to a set of habits that people do, and in return they expect certain results or outcomes.*

In his book *Atomic Habits*, James Clear highlights the 'Four Laws of Behaviour Change'.
1. Make it obvious.
2. Make it attractive.
3. Make it easy.
4. Make it satisfying.

Think about the memberships you belong to (most likely for retail companies). Which ones are most satisfying? Let me rephrase that—which ones come to mind straight away? They are likely the most satisfying. Two stand out immediately for me. One is simple and satisfying, and one is not so easy, but *more* rewarding so I'm not dissuaded. Neither are for hotels unfortunately, not yet anyway, but I can see those evolving too.

The first is for Vintage Cellars, an Australian wine retailer. Their membership model includes an app on my phone with a barcode for my membership ID, which the cashier simply scans at time of purchase. The dollars I spend convert to points which eventually convert to $25 credits, and the credits are easily seen and redeemable instantly at time of purchase. The interesting thing is, I don't really know how many points it takes to earn the credit. I think it might be 500, but that doesn't matter to me, because the model is simple and straightforward, and eventually at some point I get a tangible $25 and can spend it on a free bottle of wine.

> *Spend, receive points, get dollars discounted straight away once enough points have accrued. The details don't matter because the reward is financially satisfying and relatively frequent.*

The second membership is with Qantas, Australia's largest airline, not that I can say I remember what flying feels like thanks to COVID-19 and the year 2020! Frequent flyer memberships tend to be confusing, with points (or miles), status credits, redemptions, and tiered levels, make it complicated, but also rewarding (kind of like a video game). Spend certain amounts, fly a lot, and you'll start to unlock different levels of the 'game'. Some levels give you better seating, or access to a relaxing lounge with complimentary snacks and drinks, or more flexible booking options. These airline programs offer account access online, and you can view a dashboard showing where you're at and what you need to do to get to the next level. Most importantly, the reward of free flights and status recognition are big enough incentives to instil a high level of loyalty towards their brand. The complexity, one might argue, makes members more committed and more loyal, because memorising more than one membership can be confusing at best.

The simplicity of Vintage Cellars persuades me to shop there more often, however it doesn't dissuade me from making purchases elsewhere. I'm a fan, but not a die-hard loyal one. Qantas, on the other hand, is complicated, and although switching over to Virgin Australia is always an option, it means I'd have to start from scratch, and spend time to decipher their 'currency'. I stick with Qantas, so long as they're flying to where I need to go, and their cost isn't much higher than a similar quality airline. I should note here that as a numbers person, I prefer not to spend unnecessarily, and yet I just confessed I'd spend *more* on one airline versus another, as long as it isn't *significantly* more, despite many airlines having the identical ability to transport me from A to B.

> This is the loyalty mindset you're after. The clearest sign of a customer's devotion is in their decision to choose your product or service over a less expensive competitor, despite the cost savings.
> It comes down to trust. When your reputation precedes itself, the level of trust people have in you is the linchpin of their justification that your product is worth paying more for.

Me, an arguably average flyer, made it to Gold membership status once upon a time, and more importantly, I experienced the elevated service and benefits Gold provided. This higher level of acknowledgment goes a long way in making a person feel more respected, and is often the key component of creating more compassion and understanding in a guest when things inevitably go wrong. Delayed flights weren't so bad, because the lounge afforded me a comfortable space to continue working in undisturbed. In fact, the more times I opted for another carrier, and something did go wrong, the more loyal I became to Qantas. Jetstar is Qantas' budget airline (dubbed 'Shit-star' by those who have been marred by its seemingly volatile operations). They would cancel flights with what seemed to be an ease and frequency of turning off a light switch, optimizing revenue by cancelling one route (minutes before boarding,) then using that aircraft to add an extra flight to a busier destination. Of course, it was never explained to consumers that way, but a technical malfunction in an aircraft going from

Melbourne to Sydney could be remedied by taking a less popular route's aircraft, Melbourne to Hobart for example, and using it for the Sydney leg instead.

Consumers believe they're saving money when they book via a low-cost carrier, and on the surface it's true. We all simply want to go from A to B by the fastest means possible. Often however, these carriers make up the difference in price by charging for extra luggage, and higher fees to change or cancel a booking. They scrutinize the weight of your hand luggage to increase their baggage fee revenue, and at the end of the day you can't put a price on the time that is wasted due to a flight cancellation or re-schedule.

Once, my family and I were on our way to the airport on the Sunshine Coast to catch a flight home to Sydney, when I received a text that it had been cancelled. I started to panic about work commitments I had the next day, my children missing school and all the other arrangements that would need to be adjusted. Finally, I assured myself the airline was surely just rescheduling us for later that day, I was probably getting upset over nothing. Surely I was just over-analysing the entire situation, so I rang the airline to find out what time we were rebooked for.

"Tomorrow morning," said the agent.

Excuse me? The thought of rescheduling, finding a hotel room, and everything else needing to be done made me furious. I demanded a refund, but was told they would only issue a credit to be used on future flights. I didn't ever want to fly with this carrier again—why would I want a credit? I went round and round—they made excuses and I made justifications (*they* cancelled on *me*!) until finally an exception was made for a monetary refund if I could prove that I was pregnant and wouldn't be able to fly before the credit would expire. What an ordeal! I was angry, and yet grateful to get the money back. I am very understanding of refund policies, after all, who doesn't want to keep cash if they can legally do so? In the heat of the moment, I remembered the old saying 'you get what you pay for', and what I had paid for was a low-cost carrier—never again! The moral of the story is that *time is money*, and I'm reminded of that whenever I get inconvenienced by opting for anything simply because it's the lowest-cost option.

> Don't make life difficult for your customers if you want them to be loyal. Making people jump through hoops they don't want to jump through will ultimately push them away.

Kindness is always the better way. That doesn't mean you should give in all the time, and no, 'the customer is always right' isn't true either. However, letting go of the need to be 'right' is one of the post powerful things you can do, in every aspect of your life. In business, and in life, be reasonable. See things from the other person's perspective, be empathetic, fair and kind, and you'll set yourself up for success. You'll create an extremely loyal community, too.

8
TRAINING & DEVELOPMENT
Teach Everyone Everything

It's draining and exhausting, but if everyone working for you doesn't know everything about the way your business works, it's to your detriment. They need to understand why whatever it is they just 'haphazardly' do needs to stop, especially if it has a cost, and why other things that have a cost need to be done regardless, such as customer service, loyalty, retention and recognition. They need to understand as much as they can about *your* why and your mindset, especially if you want them to evolve, grow, or simply represent you when you're not available. Developing your second-in-command staff members helps them support your values and philosophy as much as possible, regardless of where you might be—a worthwhile investment in the long run.

Leaders with a 'beautiful mind' are just that, respected but not understood. Eventually they end up with a team who simply tries to present their superior with what they believe said leader wants to hear. They stop thinking creatively and instead try to determine what you *will approve,* attempting to predict what you'll agree to. You might think that's a good thing, but it's not, because *that's what YOU are for.* Allow me to elaborate.

> *You want a team who can think outside the box, notice the industry trends and provide recommendations—not try to be the brains you already have. You're doing a great job at that.*

You want them to feel comfortable with bouncing new ideas off you, which is why teaching, training and gifting them with everything you know is paramount. If you can do that, they'll retain your fundamental principles in the back of their mind with everything they do for your business. We've learned that two of the most essential core values for humans are to feel understood and to feel they belong. There's no easier way for your team to feel these than if they feel like they understand *you*, and that you respect and value *their* opinions too.

Recruiting

The evolution of recruiting hotel revenue and sales managers from within has always stereotypically been that reservations agents make good revenue managers, while front desk agents make good sales managers. And in many ways, that's not wrong. Reservation teams deal with all the rates, rooms and market codes and know your pricing and promotions better than you know them yourself. Likewise, front desk agents are the face of the business. They like to talk to people and make for approachable sales managers. It all makes sense.

However, lately I've been flipping the script when it comes to internal recruiting. When we get down to the basic job responsibilities of each department, I started to realize that front desk agents are the real numbers people, and reservation agents are the voice of a business. The front desk is constantly monitoring numbers, such as how many arrivals and departures remain for the day, how many rooms left to sell on any given night, and study the ratings of guest reviews. They are numbers people deep down, and have the makings for excellent revenue managers.

In contrast, reservation agents are constantly *selling* your rooms. They hear the resistance of guests when the price quoted is too high, and they know how to retain a customer through offering concessions such as loyalty member discounts. They know how to sell, and are in constant communication with your sales team already, and your clients, when they manage blocks of group bookings.

In summary, the typical in-house recruiting progression for revenue and sales positions looks like this:

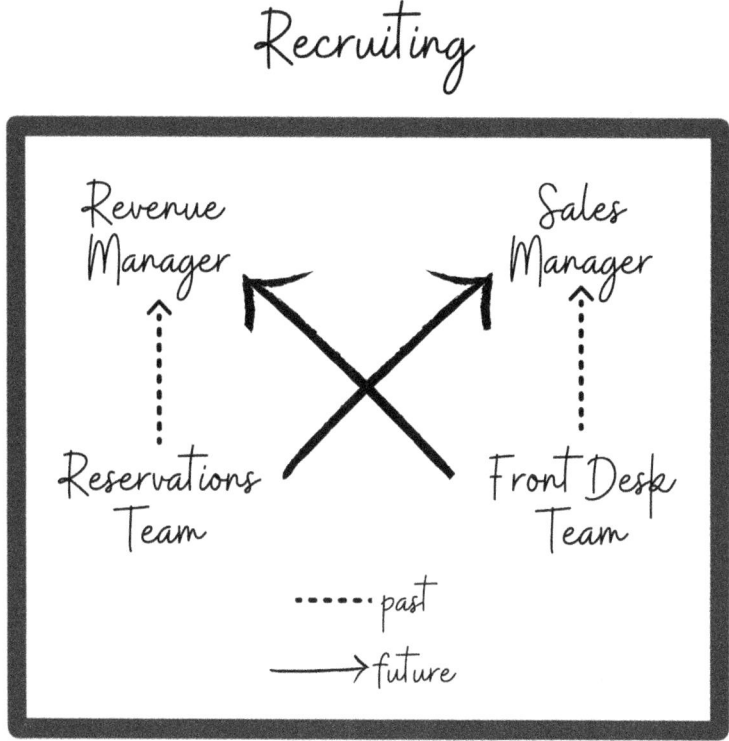

These are just starting points. It all comes down to getting the right person with the right abilities, and attitude, into the right role, regardless of what traditional experience they might have.

The Measure of Quality

Your business is only as good as your newest employee, whether they're an executive or an entry-level worker, and that includes housekeeping attendants. This reinforces teaching your team everything you know, because as the saying goes, 'sharing is caring'. Every person working for you needs to understand the core values of your business through quality training and development.

The more they know, the more they grow.

None of this means you personally need to do it all, but everyone should see you personally supporting the efforts of those who teach what you preach. As we've discussed, rock-solid service culture is imperative in any business.

Set Up for Success

When it comes to job descriptions, less is more. The right people will go above and beyond to fill in the blanks between the responsibilities as they appear in writing, and everything else that needs to be done. The wrong ones won't. In revenue management there are many qualities we want managers to possess, far beyond the numbers and spreadsheet skills. They need to see the big picture and articulate the strategies to get there in a way that makes you feel confident in their ability, which is why a Revenue Manager Success Profile, and an abilities self-assessment, are such beneficial tools for both you and your team. Not only does it serve as a checklist that ensures you're appointing a well-rounded manager, but it also allows for those interested in a particular job to understand exactly what they need to master to be considered for the role. It serves as a road map for you to mentor your eager team members and connect them with the right coaching opportunities for each of the abilities they'll require.

Having a simple job description and a detailed abilities assessment is important for any role, particularly the ones that look after your revenue.

Please understand there will always be different qualities that are more important to certain entities than others. Owners, management companies and team structures will all play a part in prioritizing abilities. In my time at EVENT, we created an RM Success Profile with the help of our People & Culture (P&C) whiz, senior revenue executives, area general managers, hotel general managers, and a revenue management consultant. I wanted a broad spectrum of input and expertise that went beyond the traditional role. Each person discussed their idea of the perfect candidate individually with the P&C guru, and later came together to defend, debate, and ultimately decide which qualities were *essential*, and which were *desirable*, for our RMs to possess.

Ultimately, it came down to this:

Revenue Manager Success Profile

Essential Mindsets and Behaviours

| Entrepreneurial & Commercial Thinking | Analysing | Deciding & Initiating Action | Persuading & Influencing | Writing & Reporting |

Desirable Mindsets and Behaviours

| Applying Expertise & Technology | Formulating Strategies & Concepts | Learning & Researching | Adapting & Responding to Change | Planning & Organising |

Within each essential mindset and behaviour, a more descriptive explanation and rating of positive and negative attributes created a template for both employer and candidate to use as a benchmark to assess and improve. Expanding on each mindset and behaviour for essential and desirable attributes then created this:

Revenue Manager Success Profile

Essential Mindsets & Behaviours

These are the essential mindsets and behaviours our very best and most successful Revenue Managers bring to their role each day. They are the mindsets and behaviours our Revenue Managers should be focused on and continuously improve and develop in themselves and the entire revenue team.

Entrepreneurial & Commercial Thinking

- Demonstrates strong financial awareness
- Controls costs and thinks in terms of profit, loss and added value
- Identifies business opportunities for EVENT
- Keeps up-to-date with competitor and market trends

Analysing

- Analyses numerical, verbal and all other sources of data
- Breaks information into parts, patterns and relationships
- Probes for information or deep understanding of issues
- Makes rational judgements from data and analysis
- Understands how one issue is part of a larger system

Deciding & Initiating Action

- Makes prompt, clear decisions which may involve tough choices or considered risks
- Takes responsibility for actions, projects and people
- Takes initiative, acts with confidence and works under own direction
- Initiates and generates activity

Persuading & Influencing

- Makes a strong personal impression on others
- Gains clear agreement and commitment by persuading, convincing, negotiating
- Effectively promotes ideas on behalf of self or others
- Strategically uses internal processes to influence and persuade

Writing & Reporting

- Writes clearly, succinctly, correctly and convincingly
- Avoids unnecessary use of jargon or complicated language
- Writes in a well structured and logical way
- Structures information for audience needs

Revenue Manager Success Profile

Desirable Mindsets & Behaviours

These are the desirable mindsets and behaviours a successful Revenue Managers brings to their role each day. While these mindsets and behaviours are not essential, they are additional areas for Revenue Managers to focus on and develop to support their success and the success of the entire revenue team.

Applying Expertise & Technology

- Applies specialist, detailed technical expertise
- Develops knowledge through professional development
- Shares expertise and knowledge
- Uses technology to achieve work objectives
- Demonstrates understanding of other roles and functions

Formulating Strategies & Concepts

- Works strategically to realise organisational goals
- Sets and develops strategies
- Develops a positive view of the business' future potential
- Considers of a wide range of issues about the organisation

Learning & Researching

- Rapidly learns new tasks and information
- Gathers comprehensive information for decisions
- Demonstrates rapid understanding of new information
- Learns from successes, failures and feedback
- Collects and shares, knowledge, resources, tools

Adapting & Responding to Change

- Adapts to changing circumstances
- Accepts new ideas and change initiatives
- Adapts interpersonal style to suit people, situations
- Deals with ambiguity, making positive use of the opportunities it presents

Planning & Organising

- Sets clearly defined objectives
- Plans work and projects well in advance and accounts for changing circumstances
- Manages time effectively
- Identifies and organises resources to accomplish tasks
- Monitors performance against deadlines and milestones

Creating a clear and concise Success Profile set both parties up with a full understanding of all expectations right from the start and avoided any misinterpretations from the original job description. They can be created for every position in your organization to provide a universal comprehension of all jobs you have within your business. At EVENT, we used the SHL Universal Competency Framework to create the core components structure for each role. The attributes are as it says, universal, and therefore translatable for every type of organisation to get started with.

Think Outside the Building

Perhaps at this point you're starting to feel a bit anxious about where to start. Where do you find these supposed ideal candidates? "How do I recruit and create and train Revenue Managers to the level you say they should be when I'm still learning too?" you ask. "If I had it all figured out, I wouldn't be reading this book!" you confess. I'm with you.

Calm down. Stop. Breathe. In the words of the highly successful, multi-entrepreneurial and now author Marie Forleo, "... everything is figureoutable." By no means did I write this book for anyone to think they aren't doing enough or need to take this all on themselves. Instead, I encourage you to think beyond the walls of your establishment, and over to the professional training and development centres that are relevant to your industry, commonly referred to as educational centres, or schools.

There are tons, and I mean tons, of learning facilities, committees, associations and courses committed to revenue management, particularly at universities and hospitality institutions, and they need *you*! A class' curriculum is only as good as its relevance to the real-world roles it's preparing students for, and they often reach out to industry associations for guidance and support on providing relevant and up-to-date information on the ever-evolving commercial world they are teaching about.

In Australia, I've provided input and feedback on revenue

management syllabus via organisations such as HSMAI (Hotel Sales and Marketing Association International) and TAFE (Technical and Further Education). Opting to share the wealth of expertise and knowledge you've gained during your career with these groups not only helps develop courses that have real-time relevance, but also gives you access to students who are ultimately going to be looking for jobs in your field in the future. No, they may not be ready to jump into a managerial role, but anyone with a revenue-oriented mindset is a good one to have on your team, in any capacity.

Creating a career path that encompasses time in every department will also create a well-balanced employee, who ultimately someday may be ready to take on *your* role. And in a perfect world, we all want someone keen and eager to learn, do, know and grow, so much so they'll be better equipped for our role one day when we're ready to step up into a more senior position, pursue a new passion, or retire. Finding those junior learners now can create an excellent array of potential leadership candidates down the track.

Outsource Training

Leaning on schools and associations for talent, and contributing to creating industry relevant curriculums, has more benefits than just recruiting. It also exposes you to the training resources available for yourself or your team. When I mentioned to a colleague that I was writing this book, she eagerly explained how I would be able to then create and launch e-learning courses and online training. That sounded interesting, but in reality there's no need, because in my opinion the endless number of exceptional courses and training that already exist for hotel revenue management is more than enough. You'll find a few examples of some excellent learning resources I've utilised on the Revenue 20/20 website (www.revenue2020.com).

When one of my former distribution coordinators wanted to consider a role as a hotel revenue manager, he came to me for guidance. I can talk about revenue fundamentals all day, and I wish I could have pushed pause on the high-level responsibilities of my role to teach him everything I know, but I knew that wasn't an option at the time. So I came up with a plan that included him spending a few hours a week at several different hotels in the group, working with and shadowing some of the company's best revenue managers, and attending a six-week course at TAFE. The course was one or two nights a week, a few hours each, and would teach him a lot about revenue. It had cost the company a few hundred dollars, and it was worth every cent. Why? Because he could see that his employer was willing to invest in his future financially, and we could see he was serious about a revenue career path by attending the course during his personal time.

It won't always work out so easily, however offering external education for your team provides more than just knowledge, it gives your employees more appreciation for the company they work for as well as the decision makers within it. Yes, someone may take a course that you paid for, then jump ship to work for a competitor. That's always a risk, but chances are you'll hire a few of those too, which is why I believe it's always worthwhile regardless. If it helps give peace of mind, you could create a mutual agreement, if the employee leaves within twelve months of attending the training they'll need to pay back some of the cost, for example. If they are loyal, and/or passionate about enhancing their skillset, they won't hesitate to commit.

Just like my decision not to create another e-learning platform, there's no need to reinvent the wheel, or sacrifice a lot of time to teach your team the fundamentals of the operations of your industry. True, many of these courses come at a cost, financially, but often they are all conducted online, or after hours. Ultimately, saving *your* time has a high financial beneficial as well. Support your industry's associations, and let them also support you.

9
OUTSOURCING

By now you might still be thinking (stressing, panicking) that there's so very much that goes into revenue management, and you aren't sure where to begin. Rest assured that the anxiety attack, or ocean of overwhelm you might be feeling right now, will be truly short-lived. In fact, by the end of this chapter you'll be reinvigorated to make magic happen. I've saved the best for last.

Outsource: verb (used with object), out·sourced, out·sourc·ing.[xi]
1. (of a company or organization) to purchase (goods) or subcontract (services) from an outside supplier or source.
1.1 to contract out (jobs, services, etc.).

Source it out - let those who do it best, do it best for you.

When I was growing up, my parents operated more like financial controllers than revenue generators. Like many children with savings-focused parents, nothing was ever purchased brand new or handed out freely. Eventually, I stopped asking if I could buy things and started figuring out how to *make* some of them instead. I was convinced if I could learn how to make everything myself, I would never have to ask for anything again.

Goodness, that was a brutal existence! Time and time again, I'd create poor quality versions of my ideas, usually admitting defeat halfway through, yet holding firm to the belief that if it existed in a shop, I could surely make something just as nice, if not better, than what I coveted from the retail world. My parents should have just let me buy a few items, get it out of my system, and focus my creativity on better things! Although perhaps they knew that once you find comfort from retail therapy it's hard to go back. Naively and eagerly, I continued to try and create that which already existed, and almost always came up with haphazard versions at best. In hindsight, if I could've understood empathy for the skill, sweat, passion and pain that went into perfecting consumer products, I would have had a very different childhood. I would have let go. Yet I also know that figuring out how to do things myself helped cultivate my problem-solving skills and enhance my autonomy. No regrets, other than time differently spent.

Thankfully, decades later, I gave in and gave up, and it was the best thing I could've done. Defeated and depleted by half-assed attempts at re-inventing wheels that took others years to get right, I decided to surrender and give credit where credit was due. I acknowledged the respect I had for every talented individual who sacrifices their time, blood, and tears to actualize their ideas, and their dedication and steadfast focus on *one passion* until they perfect their craft. These individuals have vision and focus. They don't lose sight of their destiny until they've manifested the greatness they'd intended to create all along, which is exactly what I felt when I was writing this book.

I stopped trying to do it all myself and started allowing others to help me with the parts of my life I'm not good at or loathe doing. Life is too short, and my time too precious to be depleted by a tedious task I'm struggling with, especially when there is someone out there who is more skilled, efficient, and probably even passionate about. This acceptance gave me clearer vision to notice what I was truly driven by—inspiring others to live their best lives in every way possible.

This was a pivotal moment for me, a turning point. Suddenly, as if life were flashing before my eyes, I saw all the moments of joy that ignited my ambition and gave me chills coaching, training, guiding, mentoring, supporting, motivating and inspiring those around me had always been my passion—my purpose. Creating synergies within teams, and connections with anyone interested in improving their tasks, career, health, wealth, or anything really, the desire to level up their life in some way—that's what lights a fire within my soul.

> *Had I not let go of the mundane, I would have never made room for the magical.*

Perhaps, like me, you're not good at asking for help. Maybe you worry about the cost or inconvenience that delegating will create. You might have the 'if you want it done right, then you should do it yourself' mantra, like many of us who crave full control reprimand ourselves with when things aren't done 'perfectly'.

We all have different talents, and you're perfect at yours, but the objective in life is not perfection, it's *progress*. Perfect is a mystical creature (demon) that does not exist except in fiction and fairy tales, because it can, because who wouldn't want to imagine it could be that way? You have a vast array of qualities that, combined exactly as they are within you, make you the perfect fit for the path you have right now and the course you've set your life on. This doesn't mean it can't, won't or shouldn't change—quite the opposite—it implies that acceptance of who you are and how your life is now is to let go of control and perfection, and just be. In work and in life, when you define your values and those of the business you're in, you'll begin choosing to make decisions that better align with those values. This is the magic, and how long-lasting change happens.

> *Here's the reality though—you cannot do, make or manage all the things life throws at you without a village.*

Rome wasn't built in a day, nor was it made by one man. And if you think you can do it all, I urge you to try to accept that outsourcing some of your responsibilities is a better way. It will help free up time for you to focus on aspects of your life that matter to you more than filing your own taxes. More and more business coaches and inspiring business leaders encourage delegating easier tasks to others who are capable in order to create more room to hone in on your specialty and spend more time on the parts that spark joy. After years of resisting, I'm now whole-heartedly on board, and shouting from the rooftops about the benefits of it too.

Delegating is different for everyone and every business, but as the 'sharing economy' continues to immerse itself in our lives, it's clear to see how much we outsource already. Eating out frees up time from not having to shop, cook or clean up, Uber Eats frees up the commute time of the eating out option. So much of your life is already outsourced. I'm simply suggesting you try leveraging a similar approach that just might improve revenue, and your life's satisfaction. That coffee you bought? Outsourced. The dry cleaning because you're not great at ironing? Outsourced. The electrician because the lights aren't working, the repairman to patch the wall, the auto shop to service your car, the cleaners to help you keep up with the dust bunnies—there's a village already helping you with at least one of those tasks, likely more.

Doing it all yourself provides a sense of control, I get it, but take a moment to pause and ask yourself—are you really keeping up with it all the way you would like to? Or could outsourcing give you a *meta-control* of more aspects of your life than you currently manage yourself?

I'm not a good artist because I don't spend enough time painting. I'm not a good bread maker because, as I've found out during the first COVID-19 lockdown, even keeping sourdough starter alive is not something I'm able to do. I'm not good at interior design because I gravitate towards the cost of objects instead of the 'big picture' perspective of styling a room. I've learned to outsource these things, and more, and feel great about making the decision to hand them over to experts in their respective fields instead. The bread from the bakery tastes a little more special these days, especially sourdough, and the home I live in gives me an extra dose of gratitude for entrusting people with interior design acumen to help create something more beautiful than I ever could have on my own. There's no shame in admitting you aren't a professional at a particular subject and asking for help, especially when there's so much help available and it's so easily accessible these days.

In conversation many years ago, my friend Liesl, a business development manager for a law firm, whose husband worked for a superannuation fund, described to me his responsibilities compared to her role. "Numbers don't dance around in my head like they do for Ryan," she explained. Suddenly, I had a clear image of all the numbers, reports and spreadsheets that dance around in mine and knew exactly what she was trying to say. Numbers aren't everyone's expertise, and that's okay! Everyone can be successful, glass ceilings, stigmas and stereotypes be gone. There are people, apps and software that can help each of us with our particular shortfalls, and in turn allow us to succeed *and thrive*.

It's give and take. You have a business other people are willing to give you money for, and they in turn have businesses that you give money to. That may be the most basic definition of commerce. Sometimes we lose sight of this when we're hyper-focused on saving money or reducing expense. In his book *The Barefoot Investor – The Only Money Guide You'll Ever Need*, author and financial expert Scott Pape introduced me to the idea that bringing in more earnings is ultimately what will lead to more savings or profit. Not spending money will certainly yield savings, however if the income is small, the amount you save will be inevitably small too. He gives an example about people who like drinking $80 bottles of wine every day. They are absolutely welcome to, so long as their proportions of earning, saving, spending, and splurging are all in alignment. More often than not, bringing in the experts is money well spent improving ROI, and time management too.

Outsourcing doesn't need to be expensive. Sometimes hoteliers just choose to connect with an expert consultant for an hour or two to give them advice on an idea or coach them on a particular area of their business. Maybe it's not troubleshooting they're after, perhaps a lack of quality resources in their geographical area would suggest outsourcing an entire department to an external team as the way to go. One of the businesses I work closely with and frequently recommend, Nuvho, provides complete end-to-end revenue management for hotels lacking a full-time person, yet wanting a more experienced and affordable option. One of these properties is a five-star product in Brisbane, and in conversation their General Manager endorsed their decision to use Nuvho, explaining that it was exactly as if they had their own RM with routine meetings and frequent communication. I also know of many hotels who outsource their entire housekeeping unit to an outside company, saving them time, liability, scheduling, human resources and quality control. Concerns with cleanliness therefore don't require a formal meeting with the housekeeping attendant, just a brief conversation to the outsourcing representative instead.

Reservations teams within international hotel chains are often centralized to create cost efficiencies and allow a minimal number of agents to handle a maximum number of hotels and their bookings. Once, I'd even considered outsourcing most of the high-level revenue reporting we were generating in-house to a team in India! They'd dial into our servers and copy the exact steps of completing the reports, easy! We didn't in the end, however, only because there was a greater need to overhaul the number of reports we were distributing (remember, less is more). Delegating them would have caused us to become complacent in prioritising that.

> *The option to outsource tedious tasks or reduce multi-step processes, by way of widgets and software, is becoming more of the norm these days, just ask Siri.*

Throughout my career, consultants became a fast favourite because they could be switched on and off depending on how much or how little work, spend or projects there were. Just as hotel promotions are opened over need periods and then closed once the revenue boost is achieved, consultants can be managed like that too. They don't remain open and idle online (or in their case on the payroll) if there isn't a need or they don't have work to do. With contractors, you usually don't pay them any company benefits outside of project related expenses, and you can flex your use of their expertise as much or as little as you need, whenever you need, relatively speaking.

My main go-to consultant in my years at EVENT Hospitality was a talented man named Andreas. In fact, he's now an important part of my Revenue 20/20 consulting business too. He had worked for EVENT himself for fifteen or so years, in revenue, marketing, distribution, operations, etc.—you name it, he'd likely done it. Andreas' wife was a successful doctor, they lived in a beautiful part of the world two hours outside of Sydney and had four children when he decided to 'resign'. For Andreas, it made the most sense to gain more control of his time by stepping down from a full-time role, no longer being employed by EVENT but instead consult for the very same hospitality company he knew so well. His decision meant he could flex his workload and leverage his expertise as much or as little as he needed or wanted to, while balancing what was best for his family dynamic.

To ensure EVENT was always satisfied with his work, he would go above and beyond the scope or the hours of his task to execute each project extremely well. By only having to focus on a handful of undertakings at a time, he was able to give more of his attention to the jobs at hand, without the distractions of office politics or administrative tasks. His contributions were outcome based and didn't need to be performance managed, he was autonomous. Over time, he understood exactly what each leader was expecting and delivered it with ease, becoming their go-to, 'give it to Andreas', set-and-forget kind of guy. When EVENT would sign a contract to manage a new hotel for an owner, we would send him in to help migrate all the revenue and distribution, systems and reporting setup, onto our platforms. If a hotel was underperforming, we could have him conduct a health check to provide both an external and internal review of the operational and end-user experience and provide feedback and advice accordingly.

The benefits of consultants are abundant when you engage with the right ones who integrate well with your team and your business. There's not one right person nor one correct way to leverage the skills of an external advisor, it's usually trial and error that determines the best alignment of personality and values. With Revenue 20/20 clients I'm the first port of call when prospects reach out, and I assist with matching the right field expert with the business owner or operator based on their specific needs and expectations, because one size certainly does not fit all.

Sometimes a business is looking for a solution that exists outside their box of tools. For example, a hotel revenue expert might be just what a restaurant is after to better understand how to maximise their seating capacity or occupancy in a different way. Likewise, a hotel operations executive could be the better choice to provide coaching and advice to an owner regarding his/her establishment, depending on what their main concern is. A sales management professional might provide a better point of view of base business potential at a regional property than their in-house team could. Thinking beyond the status quo always has its upsides.

> *It's important to find the right fit for your needs, and recognize they will always be evolving and changing as you continue to level up your business.*

Being able to try out an external option before formally committing them to your project gives both client and consultant peace of mind. At Revenue 20/20, I consider myself a matchmaker of sorts, pairing who I believe to be the right clients with the best-suited experts. Knowing they're only investing an hour or so of time and money puts us all at ease, because I can gladly suggest a different option if the first connection isn't the right fit. This is the method of any business interviewing employees—recognizing the candidate's skill set and potential and comparing them to the requirements of the job and how well they will align with the existing operators. This is the basic way to predict the best fit. However, unlike hiring employees, with consultants there is no probationary period or performance managing to hassle with, simply an unbiased and 'no hard feelings' decision to move on.

I've seen so many departments engage with a highly regarded expert, and sign up to high-priced and highly committed contracts, only to realize halfway through that they really weren't the right person for the job. Sadly, the contracted arrangement usually forges ahead because of the sunken costs they've already invested and inability to exit the agreement without bleeding more money. It makes me feel ill just thinking about it. With Revenue 20/20, I wanted to ensure the option of delegating or outsourcing was accessible to all different types and sizes of businesses. If one consultant isn't a good fit there are no hard feelings, we have plenty more. This means a client doesn't need to start from scratch or find another consulting company, they simply choose a different option from us instead. It also means they have the convenience of not repeating themselves, because the client's needs are communicated to the next consultant when they handover the project. This process can continue until 'the shoe fits' comfortably for everyone involved. Ultimately, that's the most important goal. With only an hour-long consulting fee for each initial session, the client's apprehension about potentially over-committing into a lengthy consulting contract is eliminated.

The owner of the bed and breakfast down the coast can rely on the same person a national chain does. Depending on the help they're after, one might require an hour of coaching assistance, and the other a month, both are viable options. Creating a dynamic consultancy that helps not only big and small, but also a vast array of teams, departments and even industries improve their incomes, is the reason Revenue 20/20 was created.

This is not a sales pitch because of course there is a downside to using consultants too. Engaging with an advisor means you're in a non-committed relationship. Yes, you read that right, you're still allowed to see other people and may one day choose to engage someone else if the other doesn't fully commit or the mutual attraction becomes one-sided. And that's okay, because utilizing consultants creates a hyperawareness towards on-going projects, workload, and spend, including whether a more permanent solution is necessary. This in turn provides clarity, and prompts prioritising the most important responsibilities above all else. Outsourcing can often be the 'try before you buy' a more permanent in-house solution, be it a full-time employee or costly software. Should you later choose to hire someone to manage the tasks in house, your consultant can be the one to provide training and handover of their projects to said newly hired employee without you getting involved—how great is that?

From time to time, Andreas would assume revenue reporting responsibilities whenever an analyst took annual leave. This meant when we hired anyone new, he would be the one teaching and explaining our systems, procedures and reporting expectations—instead of me! This allowed my time to be spent focusing on optimizing strategies to enhance our revenue generating tools and analytics at a group level instead of training someone new on old routine reporting—a win-win for all.

Sometimes outsourcing is temporary, and you use a consultant. Sometimes it's long-term and you engage with a company to handle the responsibilities of a role without the hassle, or contract a service provider for one of your departments. What if your need is bigger than that? If your takeaway from this book so far is a long list of projects and strategic reviews of your entire operation, then perhaps the solution of using a management company should be considered.

Management Agreements

A management agreement refers to engaging a larger hotel group, chain or company to assist you with more than just an idea or sanity check. They come in all shapes and sizes, and generally speaking, infiltrate every area of your business to provide advice, suggest improvements and streamline your cost of operations by using their bigger buying power. Speaking from my experience within the hotel industry, management companies are generally great and extremely helpful with growing revenues and cutting costs. I've worked with a handful over the years, big and small, and my biggest takeaway—one that I cannot emphasize enough—is that one size does not fit all. However, sometimes one size can fit many.

EVENT Hospitality & Entertainment was what I would consider to be a local brand for Australia and New Zealand. In my near ten years, we saw, pitched to and worked with a vast variety of hotels and respective owners. Everything from pub-like properties, hotels at racecourses, airports and anything in-between—nothing was too big or small for us to manage. We were the largest Australian hotel company on the ASX with the most amount of hotel rooms in our portfolio within Australia and New Zealand. Collectively EVENT owned, managed or oversaw via service agreements more than fifty hotels and 10,000 hotel rooms. We were big enough to having buying power, yet small enough to stay nimble and pivot when faced with crisis. The hotels we managed could rely on a solid corporate structure, while still knowing we were adaptable and understanding enough to make exceptions to nearly any rule.

With The Westin in Las Vegas, we had vastly different demand periods compared to our Starwood Hotels sister properties across America and most of the world. When their corporate office would roll out a promotion across all hotels, we were reluctant to participate when it coincided with our peak periods of demand. Unfortunately, more often than not, it would be insisted that we be included, despite our high rates and limited availability. The intention was to provide a compelling promotion on a global scale to their SPG loyalty members. In order to do this, they needed full participation and an identical offer setup to market a consistent message. Great for the management group, good for the loyalty members, confusing to the hotel staff and guests who didn't understand the high-level logic of being on sale when there wasn't much left to sell...

I applied all my learnings from this way of doing things at EVENT. Whenever we solicited hotels to participate in a promotion, I'd welcome them to justify why they might want to opt out. The vast geographical and seasonal diversity in the Southern Hemisphere is indicative of that on a global scale. In winter, New Zealand and parts of Australia have snowy slopes and coveted ski seasons, while Queensland touts the perfect time to visit with comfortably warm temperatures. In summer, some of these locations remain enticing for other reasons, snowboards swapped for mountain bikes for example, while others, like the northern areas of Australia, enter their hot and humid wet season and aren't as compelling to travel to. Locations where seasons vary drastically means visitor demand fluctuates significantly too.

EVENT hotels were just as contrasted with their seasons as a Starwood hotel group, which is why I rarely insisted every property participate, particularly managed hotels. How could we insist an owner should discount their revenues for the sake of our brand while paying *us* to make them *more money*? I could not, and would not, do this just as I could and would not stand in the way of revenue-generating ideas some owners wanted to try or implement at their hotel.

The stereo typical example of this was group-buying companies such as Groupon, Scoopon, and Who-Knew-pon—the-list-was-always-growing. Sure, they were a convenient way to drum up some volume of cheap business quickly, but they tarnished the reputation of the hotel's brand if the offer wasn't also offered to loyal customers booking via the hotel's own website. Hotels would reason they didn't want to offer such a cheap offer on their site, but having always felt strongly we should encourage guests to stay loyal to our brand (and site) by reciprocating the deal, I would push hard for reciprocal offers. Not doing so would encourage them to look to group buying offers every time they wanted to visit instead.

The group buying customer demographic is arguably only loyal to [what they perceive to be] a good deal. Analytics after their stay would often indicate they didn't spend much, if anything, in the hotel once they arrived. In my opinion, there were many other ways to offer low rates in a more discreet way that could also benefit relationships with long-standing distributors instead. A '$300 rate' that was discounted to '$200 promotion' price for Groupon customers, not uncommon to be contracted at a commission of 50% (50%!) for the group buying site at that time, yielded a $100 room rate for the hotel. If a hotel was willing to accept a $100 price point during an extreme need period, they were better off reaching out to their contracted wholesalers and travel agents with the offer instead. This would reinforce the relationship and allow those distributors to showcase their ability to help in times of need. If for whatever reason they couldn't produce, it would also serve as leverage to reduce commissions or allotments for next year when their contracts came up for renewal.

Nonetheless, if an owner wanted to try to generate revenue through a channel we didn't necessarily approve of from a brand perspective, while strong discussions would be had to dissuade them, ultimately we would not stand in their way or prevent them from pursuing a potential revenue opportunity if that's what they wanted to do. Most of the time, however, we were able to provide opportunity cost analytics of other hotels in our group who had gone down a similar path and sway them that way instead. Highlighting the missed revenue potential compared to their competitive hotel set, or even prior year, was usually enough to change their minds and to stick with our more strategic plan instead.

This highlights another benefit of being part of a hotel group—data analytics from other markets and sister properties gives clearer insights to better understand trends, price sensitivity and market demand beyond an owner's singular property. On a broader scale, it also allowed hotels to have access to a tool kit of best practices from an entire group and to collaborate in campaigns at a larger level.

I was adamant that the revenue teams at EVENT, whether working in the hotels, an area role, or corporate office based, were able to synergize once or twice a year in order to build their relationships with each other, enough to lean on them for help and guidance. I was cultivating a pool of internal resources, or consultants in a way, for each revenue manager by doing so. No longer did they wait for *me* to provide feedback, they'd reach out to their peers for guidance instead, because they had improved their comfort levels with doing so. I passionately believe there's always potential to further enhance a team's sense of community by instilling more gatherings and team-building workshops—never stop trying.

There will always be more we can be doing, in every facet, I suppose. While my annual summits were key opportunities to expose the field of hotel managers in attendance to our company executives so they learn of our group-wide objectives firsthand, it was equally important to allot a large amount of time to socialise, network, and build on their relationships. It warmed my heart to see spreadsheets being reviewed and exchanged between RMs, because I knew ideas were cross-pollinating more than I could ever instil with a presentation or corporate office initiative.

> This highlights one of the more important benefits for hotels of working with a management company—access to resources.

Resources

When it comes to working with a hotel group, the abundance of knowledge is endless, the collective years of experience infinite. The ideas are bountiful, and the software, systems and support for them are more efficient and affordable than a hotelier would be able to access on their own.

With EVENT, the availability of quality human resources alone was worth engaging with them to manage a hotel. I once gifted a unique Monopoly set to my boss, the head of the hotel division, but instead of the standard boardwalks were the names of all the hotels we were looking after. Fun, right? From my perspective, all he needed were game pieces with each of our Hotel General Manager's names on them, because that man had an exceptional ability to move the perfect 'player' into a newly managed hotel to 'win the game'. In other words, he was extremely talented at finding and creating the best mutual fit for all parties. If a new GM was required at one of our existing hotels, perhaps as the result of a new hotel placement, he knew how to fill roles with well-appointed people, be it internal transfers or career path promotions. He was the ultimate matchmaker between owner and operator.

Moving GMs around to different hotels gave them exposure to a variety of property types, opportunities, and problems too, of course. It allowed them to not only learn new skills, but also look at the operations with fresh eyes and implement their own best practices. It often introduced them to new owners, management dynamics, and lifted their interpersonal skills in owner relations. Putting the best of the best in a newly signed managed hotel would reassure the owners they'd made the right decision by choosing EVENT, while kick-starting the process of optimizing revenues and reducing costs with one of our seasoned superstars at the helm. Someone who already knew our procedures and would help streamline the transition was a mutually beneficial move, and a sample of the resources management groups can provide.

Local Brands

Local hotel groups or those that are well known at a domestic level, but not necessarily more broadly, are a great option for many different owners and properties. Agreements are ever evolving to be more bespoke to each independent hotel's needs. Some owners want a 'set and forget' style option, meaning they would hand over the keys and we took over from there. With these fully managed arrangements, EVENT then assessed the operations and discerned what measures could be taken to increase revenue and reduce cost through tried and tested efficiencies, while also introducing guest satisfaction enhancements. In simple terms, agreements like these tend to be structed where a management company receives a percentage of revenue, and/or a percentage of profit, as well as additional set annual fees for other expenses such as systems, licensing, loyalty programs and so on. Marketing costs might include a commission paid for bookings generated from the hotel brand's website, and signing on with a nationally prominent brand like EVENT meant new hotels could expect to see an influx of room nights from this channel.

While the fees in this example might sound extreme, when done properly, it's a sound investment strategy for an accommodation owner. Common financial benefits align all parties involved to maintain the mutual objectives of working smarter to bring in more money, and staying diligent with costs to retain as much as possible in profit. Owners understand that the objectives are unanimous—bring in more money and put more money in the bank, which makes agreeing to the terms and conditions easier to digest. When the hotel succeeds, we *all* succeed. It's also the closest option there is to "auto-pilot" for owners. With EVENT Hospitality's tenure, reputation, and proven results, it was a straightforward decision for hotels wanting a larger presence without the higher fees that generally came with the namesake of a large international chain.

It isn't uncommon for a company to propose and set performance hurdles within the management contracts. This reassures owners of the group's confidence in their own ability to achieve stronger results than the hotel was previously obtaining, while mitigating the costs of payouts if they don't hit the target. These examples describe the more premium options, which provide great results because the management teams are vested in improving the hotel's outlook as if it were their own asset. A testament to this is the number of hotels that are signed onto the same hotel group by owners who already have another property being managed by them. It is always a pleasant reassurance for the management company when an owner chooses to add another of their hotels, be it unbranded or often re-branded from another [sometimes larger international] management company. It reinforces the value of what a quality brand alignment provides. Overall, each agreement will be different, crafted to the needs and situation of the hotel, ensuring satisfaction on all sides. At the end of the day, if it doesn't feel right, don't do it.

Global Brands

Looking at large international hotel chains, I know I've so far painted them in a poor light, when they are clearly very prominent worldwide. Big brands are great for guests, and profitable for the brands themselves, just not necessarily always well suited for every individually owned hotel. Just as with a leading national or local hotel chain, international ones serve a purpose too—for the *right* hotels. If you're located in a rural or less internationally inclined area, the likelihood of an international brand on your building improving your revenues is quite low. For example, adding Marriott to a hotel in Toowoomba might sway visitors to stay there instead of a local brand, but it would not necessarily attract *new* guests to visit the area, which is what you should expect an international, or any namesake, to do. Rather, a large *national* hotel brand would best enhance a Toowoomba property's presence, because in this case domestic visitation is what comprises most of their business.

On the other hand, a hotel in a bigger metropolitan area, competing against plenty of hotels nearby, *could* be well suited to benefit from a global brand. It might differentiate it from the pack, exposing it to the vast database of the brand's loyalty members living far and wide. Arguably however, this city hotel would also benefit just as much from a national chain, particularly if local or domestic visitation is still the most dominant. International tourists (I know they don't really exist at the moment but they will again someday) can be obtained by contracting inbound wholesales or marketing through global online travel agents, and usually at a lower cost than paying for an international hotel name on your door.

International brands are helpful to guests because they can rely on their reputation of a consistent level of quality and service no matter the location they stay. These days however, universal measures such as star ratings, AAA rankings, and online review scores, provide a benchmark across the board, regardless of hotel or brand. The downside of working with a global hotel brand is the risk of getting lost in the shuffle. Sure, there's more support and structure to compensate for so many hotels, however at a property level, often you are just a number. Literally. At the hotel level, it's likely you identify yourself to the corporate support team with a property ID number. You probably never speak to or get visits from the company's senior executives, or have your opinion heard about the unique composition of your hotel by anyone high enough to make considerations about bending the rules for your hotel.

Big brands are not all bad. I know plenty of revenue executive peers at large hotel chains, and again, they definitely serve a purpose and benefit for certain hotels. I only speak from my experience of my time working at the Westin, and not feeling very supported, and that was many moons ago. The resources were difficult to find through company portals, and calls to obtain the right help person were difficult to navigate. Corporate reports were compulsory, but never explained, and I managed to ruffle a few feathers by trying to distribute some creative promotions that weren't approved. It wasn't ideal.

Back then, the GM and I had the idea to include a rental car component in a room package. I was told by corporate that it could not (and should not) be done, and it was not going to be allowed to display on our website. At a hotel level, we knew the offer was compelling to guests and beneficial to both our hotel revenue and the rental car company, we were dismayed. In the end, I found a workaround for our 'room and rental car' promotion by creating it as a 'room type' in our PMS, then overselling that room type so it would display on our website and be bookable. This wasn't the right way to go about setting it up, and poor room 311 was forever a confusion to the team ("Is there a CAR in the room?"), yet it was the only way I could configure it at the time.

All that said, I would still insist the owners of that hotel in Las Vegas were very smart to brand as an international chain, they were the right fit. The property was located just off the Strip, and for the number of Starwood Preferred Guest members who stayed, plus loyalty nights redeemed using their points, there was definitely unique market segment demand for the Westin that the mainstream casino hotels weren't receiving. Vegas has changed a lot since then, with prominent casino and boutique hotels on the Las Vegas Boulevard having international branding now. No doubt The Westin Casuarina hotel still reaps the benefits of an international brand name on its door to entice guests to stay at a property a block away from the iconic Strip.

Starwood has changed a lot since then too. Firstly, they were acquired by Marriott whose presence and reputation precede themselves on a macro scale. I'm sure they've remedied many of my antiquated complaints, however thing is for certain – stakeholders will need to consider if they want to be a big fish in a little pond, or a little fish in a big one, and make their decision accordingly.

Independent Alliances

Last but not least, another option a hotel has is to survive *and thrive* as a standalone property. Ideally, your independent offering is a unique and impeccable product that provides exceptional travel reviews and ratings online, and likely wouldn't see significant enough ROI to warrant the fees and costs associated with rebranding. Sure, a management group might be able to enhance the revenues, however depending on your size it's likely the higher costs associated would negate the financial uplift an agreement like that could provide.

It's not uncommon for management companies to have a 'distribution only' option for hotels to utilise, or 'lite' versions of their agreements that allow a collection of hotels to maintain their independence while still being a part of the group. In this case, a hotel's intention is simply about expanding their reach, and brand presence, by leveraging the broader distribution platforms of bigger hotel brand websites. This also provides exposure to the affiliate sites and databases without losing an individual identity. There are also dedicated groups who aggregate many independent hotels into one larger collective, which in turn gives each hotel added online exposure and greater buying power for lower costs and commissions. One of my revenue comrades recognised this gap and went about creating a successful hotel collective group to alleviate the downsides of being independent. I'd highly recommend this option for anyone wanting to level up their distribution while accessing tools and resources that typically only big management groups can provide.

At the end of the day, it's important to remember that one size doesn't fit all. Each situation is unique, and there are many options available to enhance hotel revenues while staying within a budget. Entrusting experienced external professionals to provide impartial advice on any big decisions, to outline all the options before making any final decisions is so important. With re-branding, licensing or management considerations, it's crucial to thoroughly review these outsourcing options with a highly knowledgeable professional in the management contract and franchise arena. At the very least, they can provide a sounding board for yourself and your trusted advisors to review proposals and compare the options of each.

Often, just engaging a trusted and seasoned industry executive who has experience working with and for different hospitality brands is all a savvy owner needs for peace of mind about their decisions. My team may not be the right fit for you, yet I guarantee there's someone out there is, and who ultimately could help save you thousands (at a minimum) in the long run.

The Takeaway

Management agreements can vary, like a restaurant's menu ranges from full degustation down to bar snacks. Sometimes hotels don't need anyone's help with costs, marketing or even revenue, they just want to increase their brand presence through a broader reach and leverage bigger buying power to reduce commission costs. These are utilised by the knowledgeable owners who understand how they could improve their exposure through hotel brand platforms at a minimal cost.

These days most hotel groups are happy to oblige with a 'lite' arrangement. It adds accommodation options for their guests and can even enhance the reputation of *their* brand as well. However, as we've explored, becoming involved with a managed hotel group is not always the right answer. Sure, it addresses how to outsource 99% of the responsibilities highlighted in this book, but as we discussed in the loyalty chapter, it isn't always necessary to achieve great results.

I'd be lying to you if I said working with a management group, or anyone externally for that matter, will be easy. Consultants and the like will provide you with unbiased observations and suggestions that may require hotels to remove certain blinders they'd been choosing to wear and face the truth. Sometimes the honest truth will mean a capital investment is required to update aspects of the business, ones that stakeholders were happier to just live with than to address with heavy spending. Advice for optimizing revenues might mean an overhaul of the trite 'because we've always done it this way' answer, to big think tank sessions of 'how can we do, be and serve better?' A new way of thinking can rattle the cages of some steadfast executives and staff of seniority who have years of experience, and possibly contributed to the original method. You'll find they are reluctant to admit that a different way of doing things could be better. Change often means hard work will be required to achieve the goals that haven't yet been accomplished.

> *In revenue, as with life, nothing good is ever easy, and hard work pays off.*

Leveraging the expertise of hotel groups and seasoned consultants allows you to create clear, concise and attainable objectives that everyone can work towards, as a team, to achieve a universal goal.

10
CONCLUSION

You've made it to the end!

Truth is, in revenue there is never really an end, and the journey itself is the reward. Numbers are black and white, but there's nothing else so exact about the rest of revenue management. The key is to keep trying different ways to generate more income, stick with what works until it doesn't anymore, then try something else. By now you have a better understanding of the basics and how transferrable they are to other industries (particularly those with perishable inventory), and to your personal life as well.

You know that numbers are critically important but have little impact without proper communication of strategies and objectives that supports changing them for the better. When you create, price and promote products, simplicity is essential for obtaining the most bookings or purchases. Using external resources to leverage your brand's visibility through broader distribution platforms, extended loyalty programs and industry association alliances will keep you relevant and recognised as a leader in your field.

You also understand that teaching everyone about everything you know is the key to consistent outcomes with your team, which will in turn deliver reliable service and optimal guest satisfaction. Guests are internal and external: The team members and departments you work with, work for, or who work for you, need just as much respect and appreciation as the ones who walk through your door and pay you for your service. Without the internal, the externals would be very difficult to attract and sustain. Never forget that *Together Everyone Achieves More* (T.E.A.M.) and the world will reward you in kind.

Kindness, above all else, will take you farther than judgement and criticism ever will, but that should not suggest that withholding truths is an act of being kind. Honest conversations will be painful, but in the end, everyone will be better off for having them.

When in doubt, OUTSOURCE! Don't spend lifetimes trying to reinvent wheels that already exist. When it can save precious time, stress and morale, getting help—either temporary or long term—is always the best option. Of course, no one likes to spend precious earnings unnecessarily, or see money go out the door on things they'd rather not have spent on, however always be mindful of what your time is worth too. Trusting professionals to do what they do best has saved many a relationship, partnership and marriage for centuries, don't be afraid to think outside the building every once in a while. We are tribal people—it always takes a village—life is too short to be unhappy and trying to do it all on your own.

If you do venture down the path of using a bigger company to help manage your operations, always remember the old adage that 'squeaky wheels are the ones that get greased'. Don't be afraid to ask for help from the corporation that has promised to guide you to better financial gains! That's ultimately what you're paying them for, their expertise, never be too proud to ask for their help. Silence can often be mistaken for contentment, which goes both ways. If you're not satisfied, say so, and remember to ask those around you, especially the quiet ones, how they are from time to time too. Help, and be helped.

Embrace diversity in every way, shape and form. Your product doesn't need to behave like everyone else's, and your team doesn't need to be 'cookie cut'. One size will never fit all, and nor would you want it to! In hospitality, and in life, there are artists and scientists. Generally speaking, revenue management and finance teams contain your scientists, while food and beverage, marketing and creative departments house more artists. Most on either side of the spectrum will never fully understand the other, and that's okay! As long as everyone acknowledges that one cannot live without the other, because both sides are vital to the vibrance of society, embracing diversity will be an enjoyable part of life both in and outside of the workplace.

You've probably noticed by now that many life lessons translate into revenue lessons, and vice versa. The funny thing about life is that there are no 'do overs'. There's no way to stop the clock, rewind and try again, no second chances that fully erase the first. The point is, we'll never know if what we've done, or not done, tried or not tried, was the hands-down best option for us or our business.

> *Trusting your gut/intuition/instinct, whatever you might call it, is the ultimate north star that guides us all. Honing in on that is a great skill—arguably the most important one there is.*

If something doesn't feel right, don't do it! But learn to recognise the difference between feelings of intuition versus those of wanting control… they're quite different. Likewise, learning to trust and have faith in your team and their ability to help you succeed means loosening your grip on perceived control and trusting your gut, and your team, in their ability to stay on course. This means letting go of the desire to be right all the time, especially the need to prove it to others—that will only feed your ego, it won't change the situation.

> *Trust the timings of your life and the path it takes you on, while always keeping a clear focus on your vision, steering your ship in that direction every single day.*

Keep learning, doing, knowing and growing. The more you know, the more you grow, and so does your revenue. Continue analysing, communicating and maintaining an open mind. Being able to pivot and stay nimble in the face of new challenges, and lean on external sources when you need help, are the ultimate keys to success. Simply to admit when you need help is a great accomplishment in itself! It never hurts to ask, so never stop questioning. And always remember that you're doing alright! That will always be more important than trying to do *all right*, because perfection is a myth.

> "Be thankful for what you have; you'll end up having more. If you concentrate on what you don't have, you will never, ever have enough."
> Oprah Winfrey

Have faith in your ability, trust yourself the most, do everything with integrity and let the numbers do the talking. When you feel lost, overwhelmed or confused, go back to the basics and start there. Stay focused on what you're doing well, applaud the great strides you've already made, and accept the facets you want to become better at. Stay positive, learn objectively from the past, and think openly about the future. Be grateful and grounded in this present moment, and the rest will follow, abundance and all.

ACKNOWLEDGEMENTS

The inspiration for this book came from many sources. My lightbulb moment was in a Chief Revenue Officer roundtable meeting several years ago. I was so passionate about a particular topic, that to me should have been a unanimous viewpoint for our industry, that I declared, "I'm going to write a book!"

I was also heavily pregnant and possibly highly hormonal at the time, which leads to my second reason—my three little boys. I still recall my first onset of "baby brain," the period where priorities shift and recollection fades. I was afraid I'd forget what my profession was outside of mothering with every birth. This evolved into wanting to detail my revenue world so that when they ask about what I do, or used to do, this book could explain everything—and probably maintain their attention longer than my verbal ramble could.

My boys were also the catalyst for accepting that continuing a full-time career in revenue was no longer my life's purpose. To analyse is to study the past, and then use those findings to predict the future. By giving all my focus to that which was, and that which might be, is to not be fully present. My passions have always been about problem-solving, creative thinking, strategy, and motivation, but over time I became lost in the numbers.

This birthed the idea of an approachable consulting business that could find out what hospitality providers need and provide problem solving with creative thinking, matching each with the ideal expert to help them stay motivated and achieve their goals. That is what I'm all about. Revenue management will always hold a special space in my heart, and I will still talk about it for hours with anyone who wants to, but now when it comes to data dicing and prophecy, I'm handing that over to my own team of experts instead.

Thank you to all the beautiful souls who live with hospitality in their hearts and go above and beyond to support and inspire in so many ways. I owe so much gratitude to my mentors, peers, friends and foes for keeping me motivated to get this book published. Writing it was the easy part—over-analysing my edits and overcoming Imposter Syndrome was a completely different story, pun intended. To everyone who held my faith, the hotels and accommodation owners who inspired me to keep going, this is for you. I hope it can help.

REFERENCES

[i] https://www.merriam-webster.com/dictionary/perish

[ii] https://www.lexico.com/en/definition/perishable

[iii] https://en.wikipedia.org/wiki/Revenue_management#cite_note-CrossR-1, Cross, R. (1997) Revenue Management: Hard-Core Tactics for Market Domination. New York, NY: Broadway Books.

[iv] https://en.wikipedia.org/wiki/Yield_management#cite_note-4, Revenue Management. Maximizing Revenue in Hospitality Operations. Dr. Gabor Forgacs, 2010. Pg. 3. Published by the Americans Hotel and Lodging Educational Institute, [1], ISBN 978-0-86612-348-8

[v] McKeown, G 2014 *Essentialism: The Discipled Pursuit of Less*, Ebury Publishing, United Kingdom.

[vi] McKeown, G 2014 *Essentialism: The Discipled Pursuit of Less*, Ebury Publishing, United Kingdom.

[vii] Ferriss, T 2011 *The 4-Hour Work Week: Escape the 9-5, Live Anywhere and Join the New Rich*. United Kingdom, Ebury Publishing.

[viii] Clear, J 2018 *Atomic Habits,* Random House Business Books, London.

[ix] https://www.huffpost.com/entry/the-power-of-writing-down_b_12002348

[x] https://en.wikipedia.org/wiki/Distribution_(marketing)#:~:text=Distribution%20is%20the %20process%20of,channels%20with%20distributors%20or%20intermediaries.

[xi] https://www.dictionary.com/browse/outsource#:~:text=(of%20a%20company%20or%20organization,bookkeeping%20to%20an%20accounting%20firm.

ABOUT THE AUTHOR

KRISTIN ROLLISON is an expert at optimising revenues in the accommodation industry. During an impressive career in Las Vegas and Australia, she worked for the likes of Starwood, Caesars Entertainment, MGM Resorts and EVENT Hospitality to maximise earnings. Now she channels her expertise and passion to help independent hospitality providers have access to the same level of expertise that large hotel chains do—the driving force behind her coaching and consulting business, Revenue 20/20.

www.ingramcontent.com/pod-product-compliance
Lightning Source LLC
Chambersburg PA
CBHW070614170426
43200CB00012B/2687